ISBN: **979865**

About Procurement

Release 1

Contents

1. Introduction

A new person was joining my team few months ago and while I was walking to the meeting room for the introductory session I thought how good it would be if I could put in writing the way I understand the procurement universe and how I like to operate so that new junior joiners can read it upfront and know how we work ahead of their first day. It was going to be a small effort at my end that could speed up things massively so I promised to myself this was not just another idea that would end up nowhere and I started writing this book.

My intention was not to build another technical book. I have created it with the aim of becoming a simple, short and hopefully very clear and helpful guide to procurement which covers the key areas and which will give to any new professional a broad idea of what we do and enable them to start operating quickly and efficiently.

I am a big fan of procurement and I think it is an amazing area to develop a professional career.

To me the business environment is a value chain in which companies transform, distribute and sell goods and services made of from a combination of natural resources and human effort.

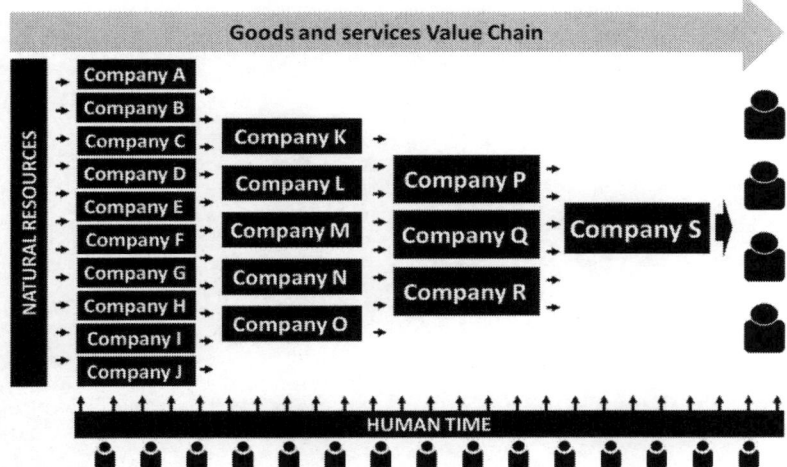

2

Everything we buy as consumers is ultimately coming from plenty of different natural resources, different transformation stages and human efforts. The resources change from one company to another until the final products or services get to the consumers. What my company sells as a final good may be acquired as a component by another company.

The role of procurement is key in this environment where there is a direct connection between profitability and efficient use of resources. Our role is to challenge and question the status quo constantly to either confirm the way we manage all non-people resources is the most valuable one or to identify improved alternatives.

I am extremely supportive of the idea that procurement plays a key decisive role in any organisation and this is what I have tried to describe in this book.

I am not an English native and although I have spent most of professional career in the UK, US and other countries, this book has not been corrected so apologies in advance for any spelling or grammar mistakes you may identify. I hope you enjoy it.

2. What is Procurement?

Procurement was historically considered the function of the company in charge of negotiating with suppliers, raising purchase requisitions and receipting invoices however from 1980s it has evolved to a much broader and strategic function.

For me the best way to define what is procurement today, is by using Simon's Sinek's Golden Circle and answering the what, the why and the how.

- **What do we do in procurement?** We run projects and ongoing initiatives to deliver value.

- **How do we do it?** By identifying, applying and maintaining commercial efficiency across the supply chain and streamlining internal processes.

- **Why do we do it?** To increase the bottom-line profit.

The above can be summarised into "procurement delivers value by ensuring commercial efficiency and improving processes to ultimately increase bottom line profit". We have highlighted 2 very interesting concepts which are value and profit. Let's see how both oh them interact with procurement.

We describe value as a judgment about how much money something is worth it. Any organisation is made of incomes and expenses with the bottom-line profit being the difference between both variables: Profit = Incomes - Expenses. How much a company is worth it usually depends on the profit so taking into account the equation above, we can conclude that the only 2 ways we have got to increase the profit and subsequently deliver value are by either reducing costs (expenses) or increasing revenue (incomes). Everything we do needs to come with a reduction to costs or an increase to revenue, if that's not the case then we won't be delivering value to the company and there is no point to carry on with the specific activity.

Some people disagree with this approach to value arguing it is too radical and we should not look at the financial component only. They say that in addition to reducing costs and increasing revenue there are a bunch of other non-financial activities that deliver value like risk mitigation, innovation, process improvement... Although I appreciate these additional things need to be a "must" in the procurement activity, I still see them ultimately translating into cost mitigation activities. Below I have listed some examples of how all the activities we do in procurement are ultimately linked to value in the way of cost reduction or revenue generation.

- **Reduce costs with third parties**: This is the most obvious activity everyone thinks of when talking about procurement. There are 3 ways we can reduce costs with 3rd parties:

  o Reduce the cost but leave the service/product as it is in terms of quantity and quality.

  o Reduce the cost by reducing the quality and/or quantity in a way that will not impact the final output.

  o Increase volume, quality, or any other term without increasing the cost. Although in this case we will be paying the same, we are getting more at the same rate.

- **Minimising risks with suppliers and regulation**: any risk, in case it happens, will translate into a cost to the company. E.g. a supplier that goes to bankrupt because their poor financial situation and we need to find alternative supply ways at a higher cost, when the regulator fines us because we are not compliant with the law or when there is a natural disaster and our data hosting provider cannot operate so we cannot make business... Risks come with a cost so avoiding risks can be considered as another way of reducing costs or at list avoiding them.

- **Resolving issues**: if issues are not resolved may turn into costs. When we don't pay invoices on time the supplier may

5

apply an interest, when goods are not delivered as agreed we may need to find substitutes at a higher cost... Resolving issues is ultimately a way of reducing costs.

- **Streamline processes**: Process improvements are normally related to 1) changing the way we do things to save resources (people's time, suppliers that will no longer be needed, facilities that can be decommissioned...) or 2 changing the way we do things to be more efficient. In both cases we will be reducing costs.

- **Facilitating innovation**: Facilitating innovation has the purpose of being ahead of competitors by developing new products (enable growth and increase revenue and profit) and creating new production techniques (reducing costs). With innovation we will also avoid incurring in massive costs in case we need to acquire new technologies when others obtain innovation before we do it.

In addition to the above there are plenty of other activities done by procurement. We could also talk about developing suppliers, gathering market knowledge, identifying new sources of suppliers for new requirements, providing support with M&As, improving cashflows... but I just wanted to list the main ones.

Understanding what value is and what is not can make the difference to become a successful procurement professional and it is something we need to ask to ourselves before we do any activity. If we are not going to deliver value, then there is no reason for us, or for anyone else, to exist within the company.

We have said the **what** is about delivering value and the **why** is to increase bottom line profit. Then we have seen some examples of **how** procurement delivers this value which mostly comes from costs savings or cost avoidance initiatives.

Now we are going to look at the other side of the value coin. While procurement delivers value mostly from cost reduction there are other teams that are focused on the revenue generation side. These other teams are normally sales and marketing and we will see below how procurement compares to them. We have defined three actions that any company can take to increase profit as well as the pros and cons and who is normally responsible of each of them.

Type of profit Increase	Action	How to do it	PROs/CONs	Timeline
Revenue Increases	Sell more	• Sales • Marketing • Production	• High costs (advertising...)	• Immediate outcomes

	Sell the same, at a higher price	• Differentiation, quality uplifts:
		  o Marketing
		  o R+D
		  o Production
			• High costs (quality increases, marketing...)	• Long-term goals

Cost Reduction	Sell with less costs	• Procurement	• Low cost (procurement resources only)	• Mid-term goals

Any improvement coming from sales normally requires much more investment than from cost reductions which makes procurement the most efficient way to achieve profit increases. This is because reducing costs normally requires man effort only whereas increasing the price of your product or increasing sales requires investment on external channels too.

The importance of procurement it is directly linked to the structure of the P&L. Procurement/3rd party spend can be up to 65-70% of the revenue depending on the industry and the company so any cost improvements have a direct impact to the net profit. In the below example we have assumed a company which breaks down its turn-over into 50% of 3rd party costs, 30 % of salaries and 20% of profit mark-up. In the column on the right-hand side, we can see how for this company a 5% reduction to 3rd party costs will translate into a 12.5% gross profit increase.

Annual data	Scenario 1	5% cost reduction
Revenue	100	100
3rd party cost	50	47.5
Salaries	30	30
Gross Profit	**20**	**22.5**
		12.5%

This is a great example to see how what apparently seems to be a small action can have a massive impact when we look at the holistic picture and analyse the bottom-line results.

So far, we have seen what procurement is and why it is so important to the organisation so let's highlight the different types of procurement and the main pillars. We will expand on them in the next chapters.

There are 3 different types of procurement depending on the nature of the goods or services we buy:

1. Direct Procurement: Relates to the acquisition of direct products that are going to be transformed (via production) or assembled before being sold to the customer. E.g. the spares required to build a car. Direct costs can directly be attributed to the final product sold by the company.

2. Product Buying: Sometimes mixed within Direct Procurement, relates to the acquisition of goods and/or services that are going to be re-sold to customers (we also call it distribution). E.g. the clothes, trainers and accessories sold by a sports e-commerce. These costs are also considered direct and they can be easily attributed to the final product or service the company sales too.

3. Indirect Procurement: Relates to the products and services required by any business to maintain its operations. E.g. travel expenses, office supplies or marketing. These costs are not directly related to production or distribution and cannot be easily accounted into the products and services sold by the company.

Some companies will have all of the above and some others won´t. No matter how many types of procurement the company has, all procurement functions needs to have at least 5 pillars:

1. **Spend Analytics**: process of obtaining visibility and understandability on the company's spend.

2. **Sourcing**: the process of deciding where and how a service or product is going to be acquired. It can be related to a new supply never purchased before or to improving existing supplies.

3. **Contract Management**: contract management is the process of creating, approving, signing, storing and monitoring contracts.

4. **Supplier Management or SRM**: the ongoing process of managing all the interfaces between our company and the suppliers to mitigate risks, ensure delivery and improve performance.

5. **P2P**: the entire process between requesting a good to making the final payment.

3. Types of procurement

What a topic! Procurement has become a very broad area in the last years. In an effort to keep things simple and with the aim to standardise a bit all the learnings I have had in my career, as seen in the previous chapter, I have defined 3 types of procurement depending on the nature and purpose of the goods/services being sourced:

1. Direct Procurement: As explained it relates to the acquisition of products that are going to be transformed (via production) or assembled before being sold to the customer. As an example, the chocolate acquired by any ice-cream producer is considered direct procurement. Not all companies have direct procurement, only those that manufacture. The cost of direct procurement normally hits the P&L at a very early stage in the way of "cost of sales" or "cost of goods".

2. Product Buying/Distribution: Normally included within Direct Procurement, as we have seen before it relates to the acquisition of goods and/or services that are going to be re-sold to customers (distribution in B2B channels, retail or ecommerce). A good example is a fashion e-commerce which acquires all type of clothes from different brands (the manufacturers), applies a mark-up and re-sells them to customers. I like to differentiate them from direct procurement because the fact that those items are only going to be stored and shipped makes them different enough to have their own category. Thy also appear in the P&L as "cost of sales".

3. Indirect Procurement: Relates to the products and services required by any business to maintain its operations. Indirect costs are not considered within the cost of sales. All businesses incur in indirect costs and they are also known as overheads.

Most of the commodities are easy to classify into direct, indirect or product but for those which may create doubts I use the below matrix

10

which basically looks at 2 concepts: 1) level of transformation made to the commodity before it gets to the end customer and 2) correlation between sales and required volume of the commodity.

Internal transformation

	High	Low
High	Direct Procurement	Product Buying
	Indirect Procurement	
Low		

(Correlation with sales — vertical axis; Internal transformation — horizontal axis)

Passing all your different spend commodities through the above matrix can give some surprises.

In the business environment, companies can be either distributors (they buy things that are sold to customers without transformation or with very little transformation), product manufacturers or service providers. Some companies can have more than one of this business roles and for example manufacture some of the products they sell and distribute some others that have been previously manufactured by someone else. Depending on the nature of the business activity the type of procurement the company will require (from the 3 we have described above) will vary.

All 3 types share common practices and processes and it is common to see individuals moving from one to the other however as detailed below there are some material differences to be considered.

	Direct Procurement	Product Buying	Indirect Procurement
Market Knowledge	o Deep market knowledge on a specific category	o Deep market knowledge on a specific category	o Average knowledge about multiple items.
Common market Challenges	o Scaccetti of suppliers. Inability to influence prices.	o Differentiation, exclusivities, high competition.	o Broad supply market. Low visibility on costs across suppliers.
Internal procurement acceptance	o High - Buyer seen as an extension of the production/R+D/ product teams.	o High - Buyer seen as an extension of the product teams.	o Stakeholders may be reluctant to partner with procurement
Focus	o Cost and quality o Availability o Deliverability	o Potential mark-up o Shipping options o Acceptability	o Cost and quality o Alternatives ways of sourcing
Technology	o Normally managed via ERP o Specific software available for stock management, MRP...	o Suppliers normally managed as "clients" via CRMs.	o Wide variety of tools- spend analysis, supplier management, e-sourcing ...
Career Development	o People move within direct procurement categories, move to other Supply Chain/Manufacturing roles or R&D roles.	o Product teams although I have seen how lots of those buyers move to sales teams at the supplier side due to their excellent market knowledge.	o Professionals tend to move across categories within Indirect Procurement or move to finance roles.

It is needed to break down procurement into the above 3 categories although I like the approach that looks at procurement holistically and promotes that procurement professionals can move during their careers to the different types of procurement so they can gain experience to manage an entire team at some point. The skillset required to be successful in procurement has 3 components: knowledge about the commodities that are being purchased, knowledge about procurement (processes…) and soft skills in the way of speed thinking, stakeholder engagement, commercial excellence and project management and prioritisation.

This means that if we develop our soft skills and get procurement knowledge the only thing that we will miss is the commodity knowledge which can be easily acquired within a relatively short period of time. When I think about procurement professionals, I try to believe it is easy to become multicategory.

In addition to the 3 types of procurement above described there is a 4th one which is public procurement. The regulation for public procurement varies from country to country so we are not going to deep into this area in this book but most of the things that will be described in here can also be applied to public procurement. The main things to consider within public procurement are:

- There is specific regulation that the professionals in this area need to follow to ensure transparency, equal treatment, open competition, and publicity of each sourcing event.

- The regulation can be at a country level or at a regional level (European Union)

- The rules normally vary depending on the amount each product/service in scope is worth it. E.g. if the product or service being request is above £18k then there is an obligation to go to tender.

- The large competitive events need to be advertised so that all kind of suppliers can participate in the tenders.

4.   Direct Procurement

As explained, direct procurement is the process of acquiring products that are going to be transformed (via production) or assembled before being sold to the customer. For example, a car manufacturer will require steal, plastics and other spares that will be part of the final car.

The goods and services procured through the process of direct procurement ultimately find their way to the end customer of the business. These goods will be part of the final product/service delivered to the customer and subsequently we will be able to attribute their costs to the final price we sell our products/services.

The main examples of direct procurement include:

- **Raw materials:** These are all the basic materials the company requires to be used in the manufacturing process to create the final product. The tomatoes required to produce tomato sauce, the chemicals required to produce cosmetics, or the bauxite require to make aluminium.

- **Semi-finished goods/components:** these are goods that have been previously manufactured by someone else and which will be used as inputs in the production process of other goods. If we think of a laptop, then an example can be the microprocessor. Rear-view mirrors for motorbikes are another good example.

The difference between raw materials and semi-finished goods can create a bit of confusion and this is because what it is seen as a raw material for one company can be seen as a semi-finished good for another. A good way to differentiate them is by thinking that raw materials are materials which we will transform in order to be part of the final product whereas semi-finished goods are goods that will just be assemble to the final product. Another way of looking at this is by thinking that raw materials are coming almost as a natural resource

14

with very little previous transformation whereas semi-finished goods have been transformed already.

Following the previous example with the aluminium, an aluminium-producer will classify aluminium as their final product and bauxite, caustic soda and lime will be the raw materials they need to produce it. Then a can manufacturer will classify the aluminium as the raw material that will be transformed in conjunction with cooper, magnesium and silicon to produce the final aluminium cans. Finally, at the other edge of the chain we have got the soft drink producer which will buy cans as semi-finished goods to add them to its production process and create the final drink that will be acquired by the customer.

- **Packaging:** packing are all the different layers we will require in order to get our product/service to the customer. There are 3 types of packaging:

  o **Primary:** packaging which is in direct contact with the product itself. E.g. for a soft drink, the primary packaging will be the can. Primary packaging will always be taken home by the customer.

  o **Secondary:** this packaging is used to preserver and transport individual units into packs of various units. Secondary packaging may or may not be taken home by the customer. E.g. for soft drinks it will be plastics or cardboard can pack

  o **Tertiary:** It is used to manage the transportations of numerous units of product. It its normally not taken home by the consumer as this includes things like corrugated boxes that will carry can packs and will be transported in pallets…

Once again it is important to note that this varies from company to company. Some companies may only have Primary packaging and some others may only have tertiary. It really depends on the product they produce and the market they operate. We can also have all packaging or tertiary packaging within indirect procurement instead of direct.

15

- **Logistics:** logistics is a very broad area that really varies from company to company but we can define it as the function in charge of transportation of inputs into the production process, outputs to the distributions channels as well as managing all the storage required across the end to end chain.

When we take raw materials, semi-finished or finished goods from an external provider into our facilities we call it inbound logistics, and when we deliver our final product to the distribution channels, we call in outbound logistics. The transportation can be done by many channels: air, sea, road or rail. Then within each channel there are multiple options. The role of procurement is to support selecting the right channel and mechanism for each logistic operation (own fleet, external supplier…) as well as continuously improve its commercial efficiency. For some industries small deviations to the logistics costs can make the difference between earning or losing money.

Logistics is a category that sometimes is part indirect procurement and some other seats with directs. It really varies from company to company.

- **Third Party Manufacturing (TPM) / Contract Manufacturer:** Companies may choose to outsource part or the entirety of the production of their products to third parties. This will mean that the third party will produce under our label or our brand. This model is used in all type of industries and it is very important to manage closely the relationship with the supplier and monitor performance to ensure quality as well as supply availability. Some of the advantages are:

  o The third-party manufacturer has lower costs due to economies of scale or because of being based offshore.
  o Transforming a fixed cost into a variable one.
  o Having more flexibility with demand picks.
  o Ability to focus on core competences.
  o Easier and cheaper market access for new products.

16

o In the last years the option of contract manufacturers directly shipping the product to customers "drop-shipping" has become very popular.

The fact that direct materials are part of the final good makes the role of procurement extremely relevant. We can split the activities into strategical and tactical.

Strategical will cover most of sourcing and SRM including the below:

o Procurement is responsible for the sourcing activity which requires to actively look for cost synergies by negotiating with existing suppliers, find alternative suppliers with better rates (maybe offshore) find alternative products and mitigate any cost increases due to increases to the cost of raw materials. It is very common to link part of the cost to a price index that establishes the cost of raw materials so that both, the company and the supplier, are protected in case of major fluctuations.

o Procurement in addition to sourcing goods will be the responsible of providing visibility to the company around the production cost of each product so that sales and pricing strategies can be effective.

o The procurement team will be an active part of the new product development process. They will work with marketing and R&D for new product development and their role will be around feasibility of the new products, cost viability as well as finding the right suppliers at the right cost.

o Procurement will also work with production and distribution to make sure the products are fit for purpose, delivered as per the agreed specifications and within the agreed timings. They will also sortin out any major issues that may happen.

o In addition to the above procurement will maintain a robust SRM process (Supplier Relationship Management) for core suppliers as well as strategies to find alternative suppliers if when suppliers fail or the market circumstances change.

Tactical is mostly around managing stock levels, sending requisitions to suppliers as well as managing the transportations of the goods. In some organisation it is done by the same team and in some others (larger normally) this bit is done by other teams.

Once a year, around Q3/Q4 all organisations create their budget for the following year which contains the expected revenues/sales and costs. Creating an accurate budget is key because on one hand will give a view on where the company will be in the next 12 months (external investors require this) and on the other hand will settle clear objectives. Direct procurement plays a key role in this process because will provide inputs about the expected costs of each product to support the sales estimations and the pricing strategies. Any fluctuations to the cost of the materials needed to create a product will be translated into either an increase to the price we sell our products/services or to a reduction to the margin we get.

5. Product Buying

Product buying or distribution procurement is the process of acquiring products and services that are going to be re-sold to customers without any transformation or with very little transformation.

It is sometimes included within direct procurement as "finished goods" however I think there are enough differences to have it separately because the buyer's behaviours and activities are different.

While within direct procurement/manufacturing, the cost of the final product sold by the company is driven by the cost of making it, in the distribution/retail/product buying area the cost of what we sell is driven by the value the customer perceives which will trigger whether the customers want to buy it or not.

Customer's perceived value is a key concept in here and it is linked to 2 factors: the customer expected benefit of the product and the cost of the product.

We have seen that in direct procurement we will always talk about value but within product buying we talk about perceived value. The subjectivity applied by the end consumer it's what makes the difference between the. We can say that while in product buying the buyer cares about market acceptance and potential price to customer, in direct procurement they care about quality and cost. In product buying quality is not a key driver itself because we may find customers interested in all levels of quality so the key driver is to identify what are the market needs and what are the most valuable products we can sell to meet those needs.

I did a piece of work for a technology retailer around their product portfolio and how to create a guide with best practices for their buyers. Using the MP3s category as an example, we assessed 2 specific products. The first one was an MP3 produced in China under a local non-well-known brand. The cost of it was £10 and the selling price was £40. It had one of the largest mark ups in the company (300%).

The other product was a very well known, US designed but China manufactured, colourful MP3. The cost to the company was £250 and selling price £300. If you think of that the Chinese solution is a much better investment so if we were talking about direct and indirect procurement, the specifications of both MP3s were similar and the supply risk was similar too, we would always have chosen the cheaper option. In product buying instead, this is very different and both products needed to be in the portfolio because there was a demand for both of them. People buying the expensive one were not interested in the cheap option and the other way around. The focus in this instance was about identifying what are the items required by our consumer and then acquiring these 2 very different items at the right costs. It is all about perceived value and expected benefit. Different people have different needs.

Within product buying the buyer's decisions are dictated by trends, fashions and the need to offer customers something different from their competitors. The buyer behaviour needs to follow the customer's behaviour, so the product portfolio needs to be defined by trends and fashions with the desire to offer customers something different to their competitors

Another good example is when a company decides to sell something with a very reduced mark-up or with no mark up. This can happen if we think the specific product will drive additional traffic for cross selling or increased reputation and awareness.

The way I understand product buying is as if buyers need to be more focused on expected acceptance and mark-up rather than the actual cost of the products. Assuming mark/ups are the same percentage, we can say that the less the customers pays for a product the lower profit we end up making.

We can think of this type of procurement as if it is more about selling than about buying. Some of the technical particularities that product buyers will put emphasis on are:

- Adequacy to market

- Competitors offering
- Stock availability
- Shipping options: drop shipping, warehouse delivery...
- Returns
- Exclusivity
- Payment terms

A side from the difference we have already mentioned, the rest of buying activities are very similar to direct procurement. Product buyers are in charge of managing the relationships with suppliers, negotiate rates and contracts, do site audits, manage performance, ensure availability and actively participate in the product development process.

Examples of product buying can be the food acquired by a supermarket, the clothes acquired by a fashion e-commerce or the insurances re-sold by an insurance broker. Unless we acquired them directly from the manufacturer all the products we buy as consumers have been procured by a product buyer or by someone acting as a product buyer without knowing it.

Every time we buy products or services, we are indirectly connected to a procurement professional. If I buy my trainers directly from the Adidas store, then the closets connection with procurement is the Adidas direct and indirect procurement teams in charge of buying all goods and services required to put those trainers into the store at the right price for me to acquire them. If instead I decide to buy them from a multi-brand sports retailer, then the closest connection with procurement will be the product buyer of this retailer in charge of the acquiring the trainers.

Product buying is normally also structured within categories. Using the same example, the sports retailer may have specialised procurement people for each category – E.g. by sport: running, cycling... or by type of item: clothes, shores, peripherals...

Sometimes product buying does not depend on procurement and it may even be managed by teams without the procurement label. It is very common in the ecommerce world that it is done by product managers however the approach should be the same.

One of the particularities of product buying is that they may have different pricing models and pricing terms than the other types of procurement.

Regarding pricing models there are plenty of options. From the most common one which is paying to the manufacturer the items that we are going to re-sell, or the less common ones like getting the items for free from the manufacturer and then getting a commission when we sell them.

Regarding pricing terms, it is important to decide whether we buy the items upfront, and take the risk of don't sell them afterwards, or whether we receive them from the supplier at no cost and we pay them only after they have been sold.

Two other key things to take into consideration are shipping options and returns.

6. Indirect Procurement

Indirect procurement relates to the management of commercial efficiencies across the indirect spend which is made of the products and services required by any business to maintain its operations. Indirect costs are also called overheads and they are not considered within the cost of sales.

Indirect products/services acquired by the company are not sold to the customers (as it happens with product buying) and are not transformed as part of a production process to create the final good (which is the case of direct procurement).

This is a very material difference because it means that increases to indirect costs cannot be easily absorbed by increasing the final price of the product or service sold by the company. They will translate into a reduction to the profit.

Some good examples of indirect goods are advertising costs, technology or real state. It obviously varies depending on the company but some of the main categories we can find within indirect procurement are:

- Marketing
- Technology
- Corporate services
- Travel
- HR related costs
- Real state / property related costs
- Utilities
- Logistics (if is not within directs)
- Maintenance Repairs and Operation (MRO)

The indirect spend can be classified in 2 types:

- **Corporate Expenditures (Capex)** – Capex is incurred when acquiring goods (assets) which benefit will last for more than 1 year. E.g. when we acquire new machinery or a new building with the aim of using it for 5 or 10 years. It also refers to any upgrade made to existing assets. The main particularity is that the cost of these assets can be amortised over a period of time which means that even we will be paying the assets on the day we acquire them (it does not help with cash flows), we will be inputting them into the P&L in equal annual instalments over the life of the assets which reduces the pressure on the P&L.

- **Operational Expenditures (Opex)** – These are all the costs the company incurs to operate on a day by day basis. Things like electricity or travel expenses.

It is very important to identify what is indirect spend and what is not because sometimes certain spend items are included within indirect when they shouldn't. The approach to manage directs and indirects varies significantly and it is crucial to set up teams in the right way. The best way to classify spend commodities is by seeing if the cost can easily be apportioned to the final product we sell. In case it can then it is direct or product buying and in case it cannot, it will fall under indirect.

The main differences between indirect procurement and the rest are:

- **Size:** Indirect procurement can be as large or larger in terms of spend than direct procurement or product buying.

- **Bottom line spend impact:** this cost in not normally directly linked to sales so it is often not taken into consideration by the budget holders at an individual level. Understanding the ROI of indirect spend when possible is key to improve commercial efficiency.

- **Supplier base:** the supplier base for indirects is normally made by a much larger number of smaller suppliers. This creates a big long tale made of lots of suppliers with very little spend which is difficult to manage.

- **The stakeholders:** the stakeholder may be reluctant to partner with indirect procurement because they can take it as if someone is interfering into their businesses. In direct procurement or product buying, procurement is one of the main decision makers and may hold ownership on the budget while for indirects, procurement acts as the advisor that supports the rest of the functions to take the right commercial decisions. Procurement will work with IT to select the right software, with marketing to select the right creative agencies and with legal to find the right legal firms. In addition will create business cases to assess "make" vs "buy" options, offshoring vs local suppliers or the use of technology to automate tasks. The fact that the ultimate budget holder is part of a different business unit which is not procurement may create a bit of tension. The stakeholders have the right business knowledge but sometimes may lack resources, the groupwide view, or commercial acumen to maximise the decisions. The goal is to avoid maverick spend which comes when the business unit bypasses procurement to source specific items by their selves.

All companies no matter their size or nature have indirect costs whereas not all of them have direct or product buying. The role of indirect procurement has increased in the last years due to the digitalisation, the increase of the services industry and the creation of large multi-country corporations. Indirect procurement is now a strategic core function due to:

- o **Scope:** it hits all areas of the organisation. From IT to Facilities. Even when raw materials used in production are not part of indirects, the rest of things required to manufacture are included (machinery, energy, temporary staff...).

25

o **Holistic approach:** Different business units or markets within the same company may be buying the same items to different suppliers. Indirect procurement provides the group view which is key to optimise costs and consolidate.

o **Bottom line impact:** As discussed in previous chapters, a reduction to costs is the easiest and cheapest way to increase profit. Bearing in mind indirect costs cannot be easily translated into price increases, failure to negotiate good contractual rates and terms and conditions across these areas can have a significant negative impact the company's P&L.

o **Quality and risk management:** Quality issues with indirect suppliers or risks potentially created by suppliers can create operational alterations that can ultimately come with costs.

o **Contract negotiations:** The ability to negotiate the right contracts with the right terms (payment terms, remediation payments in case of failure, liabilities, non-competition...) can improve the profitability, cash flow and be a source of competitive differentiation. Contracts are very relevant in indirect procurement.

In direct procurement and product buying, the byers are really specialised in a very niche commodity while within indirect procurement the scope is broader, so buyers need to have the ability to manage a wide variety of products or services. The number of suppliers is much larger than direct suppliers and the number of projects each buyer can run is also higher.

It is a very challenging role that to be successful requires a lot of strategic/long term thinking, ability to influence stakeholders, managing many projects at the same time and excellent commercial acumen.

7. Procurement 5 pillars

The number and nature of procurement sub-functions varies from company to company but in my view, there are 5 core pillars that are common to all types of procurement (direct, indirect and product buying) and that I have seen in almost all the organisations I have worked for:

1. Spend Analytics
2. Sourcing
3. Contract Management
4. Supplier Management
5. P2P

These pillars also constitute the basic knowledge and skillset anyone who wants to develop a senior career in procurement is expected to champion. We will spend a chapter for each of them but let's see quickly what they cover:

1. Spend Analytics:

Spend analytics is the process of obtaining visibility and understandability about the company's spend with the objective of providing useful insights to be used by senior executives to take strategic decisions and by procurement leaders to identify potential issues and opportunities.

We divide spend analytics in 2 stages: data gathering and data analysis. Stage 1 is about putting together in a unified way all the spend data for a specific period and it is normally done by pulling out reports from the ERPs or via automation through integrations. It is crucial to get accurate data otherwise the outcomes won't be reliable (specially in multi market/brand companies). Once we have got the data ready, stage 2 is all about analysing and visualizing it. This part of the process can be done with a wide variety of tools. From the most basic Excel type tools to the most innovative procurement specialised software some of which includes artificial intelligence and machine learning.

27

2. Sourcing:

Sourcing is the process of deciding where and how a service or a product is going to be acquired. It can be related to a new supply never purchased before or to improving existing supplies.

The main objective of sourcing is to find the right balance between the requirements (quality, availability, deliverability...) and the costs.

A standard sourcing process includes assessing the purchasing needs, mapping out a plan, conduct market research, identify the potential suppliers, negotiate final services/product terms and rates and create and sign the contract. The sourcing process can require competition in the form of RFPs or RFIs or can be a direct negotiation with a single supplier.

The sourcing team can also work as an internal cost efficiency consultant. In addition to evaluating new suppliers and improving the existing ones, sourcing also run cost efficiency projects such as: case studies around make vs buy, offshoring options, tax efficiencies, automatization... We will see this in detail in the Sourcing chapter.

Most companies/authors differentiate between Tactical Sourcing (low value low risk easy to source commodities) and Strategic Sourcing (high value, high risk or complex to source commodities).

3. Contract Management:

I understand contract management as the process of creating, approving, signing, storing and monitoring a contract. Contract management is accountable for the creation of templates (in conjunction with legal), the electronic signature systems, the online repositories that will allow the company to closely monitor terminations, payment terms, values... as well as any required reporting. Contract management is not responsible for the negotiation of the contract terms with suppliers which should be done by legal with help of the sourcing managers when required.

4. Supplier Management:

Supplier management or supplier relationship management (SRM) or Vendor Management is the ongoing process of managing all the interfaces between our company and the suppliers to:

- ensure the suppliers deliver at the agreed quality and quantity levels (performance management)
- ensure the supplier delivers at the agreed costs (commercial management)
- monitor the non-financial terms of the contract
- develop the supplier to improve delivery (innovation, efficiency...)
- mitigate potential risks (risk management)

The main activities done by SRM are assessing supplier risks, monitoring performance and developing the relationship to make it more efficient. Depending on the organisation and the size of the supplier the above tasks are done by a single team or various ones. For large suppliers it is common to have multiple supplier managers. One will oversee qualitative performance, another one will monitor commercials, another one will assess risks and so on. As a general rule we can affirm that procurement will at least be the one setting up the corporate supplier management framework and managing the systems required to undertake an accurate SRM. The specific activities will then be handed over to the BU, compliance, risk, or any other teams....

5. P2P:

P2P covers the internal end to end process between requesting a good to making the final payment. Depending on the good/service and the company, this process follows different stages however the most common ones are: Raise the request internally and get budget approval, create the Purchase Order and send it to the supplier, receipt the goods/service (not applicable to indirects), receive the invoice and receipt it, and finally make the payment. P2P is one of the areas that first adopted technology in procurement. The P2P process is normally a subsequence of the sourcing one. While sourcing is in charge of deciding what is the best way to source a service/product, P2P is the operational arm that manages the day to day purchase requisitioning. It is quite common that P2P seats with finance instead of procurement.

From my experience the way these 5 pillars are settled and managed internally varies a lot between companies. Some companies leave everything with the same team and some others have specialised procurement teams in charge of each of the pillars. I have also seen examples where P2P was managed by Finance, Contract Management was managed by Legal, SRM by compliance and Spend Analytics was run by the BI team which left procurement only with Sourcing.

In addition to the 5 pillars of Procurement we need to make a special mention to Strategy or Category Management.

As any other function procurement also requires a strategy. In companies that operate procurement functions structured by the type of spend (e.g. Marketing, Chemicals, IT…) this is normally called Category Management. Category Management is the next step to sourcing and it is about looking at the entire spend category holistically so that all the sourcing activities are aligned with the business goals. Category Management requires the teams to hold strong understanding of the commodities in scope and market trends, maintain ongoing spend review and supplier management programs and build the mid/long term strategies for each of their categories. All the category strategies will then be consolidated into the company's procurement strategy which needs to align with the business goals and ambitions.

The below table states the main responsibilities included within each of the procurement pillars although it depends on the company and the stakeholders.

		DOs	DONTs
PROCUREMENT	**Spend Analytics**	• Gather spend data and load it to the spend analytics system • Analyse main KPIs	• Invoice reconciliation • Budget allocation
	Sourcing	• RFPs, e-bit… • Price negotiations • Efficiency projects • Opportunity identification • Material issues resolution • Negotiate contractual terms	• Raise POs • Monitor supplier performance
	Contract Management	• Maintain and update contract templates • Upload contracts to inventory • Monitor terminations and spend	• Negotiate/amend contractual terms • Monitor qualitative and commercial performance
	Supplier management	• Qualitative and commercial reviews • Risk assessment • Improve relationships with suppliers	• Amend contracts • Negotiate with suppliers
	P2P	• Raise POs • Receipt Invoice • Onboard suppliers • Manage Payments • Administrate catalogues, buying syndicates and manage internal e-ordering	• Negotiate prices with suppliers • Manage budgets • Resolve issues with suppliers • Review contracts
	Category Management	• Ongoing analysis and strategy • End-to-end procurement process overseeing (all 5 sourcing pillars) • Demand management • Senior stakeholder engagement	• Run Sourcing events • Create processes and systems for the whole procurement team

8. Spend Analytics

Spend analytics or spend intelligence it's a must in any successful procurement function. I like to describe it as the eyes without which procurement is blind and cannot operate efficiently and effectively.

As briefly explained earlier it is the process of obtaining visibility and understandability about the company's spend with the objective of providing useful insights to be used by senior executives to take strategic decisions and by procurement leaders to identify issues and opportunities. We have defined below the steps to build a robust process:

1. Obtain the spend data: data gathering can be a very tedious exercise. When we have got multiple countries, with multiple ERPs and multiple currencies, accuracy is key to obtain a valid solution. Some of the considerations to make when gathering the data are:

- Make sure the currency is standardised.
- Make sure all the data follows the same pattern regarding inclusion or exclusion of VAT and other applicable taxes.
- Ensure the data is pulled out on invoice date instead of payment date to avoid issues with payments terms.

2. Taxonomy and data classification: The taxonomy is the matrix that will contain the different spend categories and will allow us to analyse the spend by the type of commodity. It must have enough categories and subcategories to be able to cover every single item and service acquired by the company. It is bespoken to each company, but I advise it to contain at least 3 levels. Se below an example.

Level 1	Level 2	Level 3
Marketing	Media	Media Agencies
Packing	Primary Packaging	Plastic Bottles
...	...	...

Once the taxonomy is created the next step is to classify all suppliers (allocate a category to every single supplier we have got in the spend data). If it hasn't been done before this task can become a massive effort. The average FTSE100 company can have approximatively 10,000 active suppliers. This means that someone either internal or external will need to go one by one through each of them and assign the right category. Without classifying the suppliers there is no way we can build a spend analytics tool because we won't be able to filter by type of spend.

3. Platform Selection: the platform is the tool where the spend data is going to be processed. It can be done with non-sophisticated systems like excel, with data visualisation tools or even with software specifically designed for spend analytics.

4. Analysis: This is the process of loading the data into the platform, monitor main KPIs, creating dashboards and analysing variation vs last year, seasonality, deviations to budget…

If done well, senior leadership will be very interested on the reports coming out of spend analytics and will be constantly asking for new reports or bespoken information.

The next stage once it is up and running is to improve KPIs and create ratios to take spend analytics to a level where it is used by top leadership to take strategic decisions. These ratios can be created combining data from other sources. Some examples are:

- **Cost income ratio:** total cost exc.HR incurred for any unit of money the company makes.
- **% Spend under contract:** spend which suppliers have a contract / those that haven't one
- **Free cashflow:** amount of cashflow generated by the company after deducting costs

9. Sourcing

Sourcing is the process of deciding where and how a service or product is going to be acquired. It can be related to a new supply never purchased before or to improving existing supplies.

In today's procurement world it is important to differentiate between Strategic Sourcing, Tactical Sourcing and Purchasing.

Strategic Sourcing is a mid/long term exercise that will set up the basis in which a product/service is going to be acquired (suppliers, contract, price...). It is focused on large, risky and strategic commodities.

Tactical sourcing is normally used to describe more short-term, non-risky, non-high value, non-core sourcing exercises.

For both of them, the sourcing managers will assess the best options to source the products/services. They will find the most valuable supplier in the market or negotiate with existing ones, agree the price and the rest of the terms and get the contract signed. Once the contract is signed then the Purchasing team will come into action.

Purchasing, which is the first step of the P2P chain, is the actual process of acquiring goods and services. The responsible for purchasing is in charge of the operational acquisition of those goods/services. This normally includes doing the ordering, raising POs, manage the inventory as well as maintaining the day to day contract with suppliers.

Sourcing tends to be more strategical while purchasing is more operational. Sourcing is about setting up the high-level basis of how something will be acquired while purchasing is about managing orders, and POs working under the basis set up by the sourcing process.

Once have clarified the way I understand the semantics around sourcing (please note the above it is just the way I see it and other people may disagree) it's time to focus on the sourcing cycle.

Every time we source a commodity, we need to go through a sourcing cycle. There are plenty of different sourcing cycles on the internet and literature, but I like to keep it very simple and divide it into 3 steps only:

1. Analyse the request
2. Create the Strategy
3. Implement the strategy

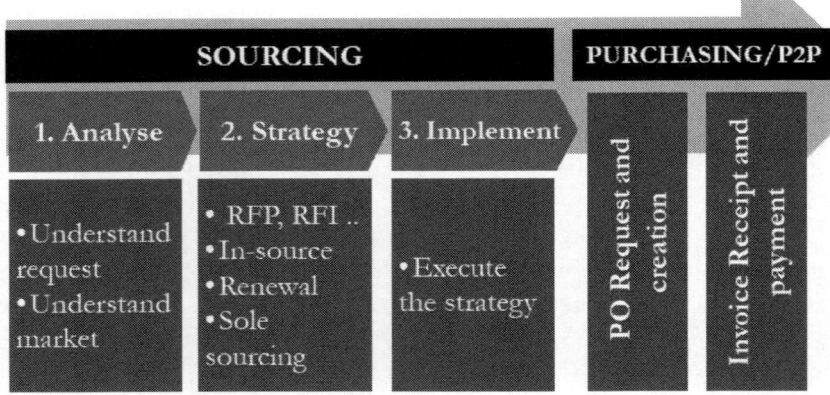

In this chapter we will only see in detail the 3 sourcing steps. The ones for purchasing will be covered in the P2P module.

1. Analyse the request: this step is about understanding what we are going to be buying and why are we buying it. It also includes market analysis.

- **Service/product specificities:** there is no need to be a subject matter expert in the specific commodity but sourcing managers at least need no know well what are the cost drivers (will see more of this in the commercial excellence module) as well as why does the company require the specific product. It is the role of the sourcing manager to challenge the quality and quantity forecasted by the business unit to ensure we are not under or over specifying. It is also important to understand the

35

emergency of the requisition so we can prioritise accordingly. Some of the questions we need to ask to ourselves are: what, why, how much, when…

- **Market conditions**: the current market conditions as well as trends of the specific commodity are key. Lack of market availability may require overstocking, or the release of a new substitutive technology may require to don't overcommit because the price of the current technology may go down in the near future. In addition, understanding what our competitors are doing from a sourcing perspective may give us some useful competitive benchmark.

- **Wide view:** One key point in here is to contextualise the request with the rest of the company's needs. It is the role of sourcing managers to identify if similar services are being acquired by any other area of the company and if there are opportunities for consolidation.

2. Create the sourcing strategy. Once we know the request it is time to select a sourcing strategy. Sometimes we won't have many alternatives due to monopolised markets or to short timelines. When creating a sourcing strategy, we need to decide whether it will be competitive or not however there are other things to take into consideration. Below some of the key things to consider when building a sourcing strategy.

- **Sole sourcing / negotiation with existing supplier:** This option avoids competition. When it is related to existing suppliers it is normally due to a renewal or an amendment to the current terms. Sole sourcing happens when a supplier has a unique proposition that cannot be found anywhere else or when we decide to avoid competition due to not expecting enough value out of it. Renewing or amending contracts with existing suppliers may be due to knowing we already receive great value, to a lack of time or to a monopoly. For all instances, it is still required to build a plan and to prepare the negotiations upfront. We need to create a story that allows the suppliers to feel part of our business and react accordingly.

- **Competitive exercise (RFP, RFI…):** Competition is about getting at least 2 suppliers to submit proposals for a specific service/product, compare them and select the most valuable one. We will see an example of a competitive exercise below but the main objective of competitive processes is to either find the best supplier for a new service/product or try to improve the value we get from our existing suppliers. Going for competition is not as easy as selecting some suppliers and ask them to send some quotes. We will see in the next chapters how there are multiple facts to be considered and multiple options to be assessed.

- **Insourcing (make vs buy)/ Outsourcing:** There is also sourcing activity that is not directly linked to competitive exercises or negotiation with existing suppliers. This is about analysing alternative ways of supply services and products like insourcing or outsourcing. We will see more of this in the Commercial Excellence module.

Sourcing processes may not finish with a fixed price or a fixed supplier. In product buying for example, a sourcing process may end up with the discount the supplier will apply to each of the items of the catalogue, the terms of the delivery (drop shipping…) and the details of the returns. Then it will be passed the purchasers who will select the portfolio and order the products as required.

In indirects, the outcome of a sourcing process may be the creation of a catalogue wherefrom all the employees will be able to order products (e.g. office supplies) or a poll of suppliers.

Sometimes the best option is to a "do nothing" strategy. We need to keep in mind that procurement exists to deliver value so if there is no way we can add value we may decide to don't be part of the process. Examples of this are a low risk and low value requests for which we know there is no better option than the existing supplier or a high value service for which we know we will face cost increases if we open the door to discussion.

Implement the strategy: depending on the strategy we select, the operationalisation will vary but in all cases a plan needs to be created identifying the different stages, timelines and roles and responsibilities. Even if it is a renewal with the existing supplier, it is crucial to articulate it in a plan. We have seen how when building our strategy we can select from a wide variety of alternatives like sole sourcing, in-sourcing, or competition amongst others however, in this chapter we are only going to see in detail the implementation/operationalisation of a standard competitive exercise (RFP, RFI...). How to implement sole sourcing strategies will be discussed in the negotiation chapter and insourcing, outsourcing and sourcing options will be covered in the commercial excellence chapter.

Once we have defined the specifications and we have selected an RFP as the strategy to follow, the next step is to operationalise it, and said before, it always starts with a plan. A standard competitive RFP process has the below steps:

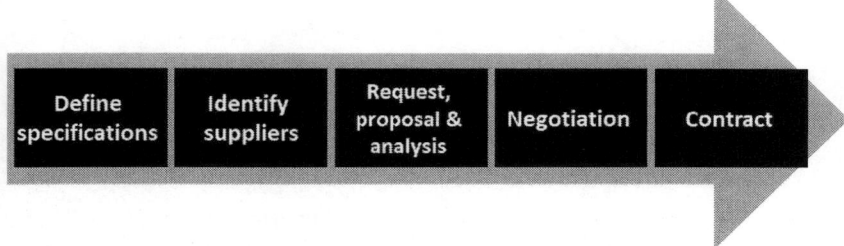

| Define specifications | Identify suppliers | Request, proposal & analysis | Negotiation | Contract |

1. Specifications: Any RFP process starts with detailing what are the services or products required to be acquired and to do so we need to create the specifications. Specifications are statements of requirements to be satisfied in the supply of a product or service. It is the role of the sourcing manager to challenge the business unit in order to ensure the quality, quantity and deliverability of the product or services it not under or over valuated. It is also the role of the sourcing manager to ensure the specifications are clear and will be clearly understood but the suppliers.

There are 2 types of specifications:

- **Performance/functional**: this happens when we don't know what we do exactly require but we know what issues the product or service needs to solve. In this case we will explain the issue we expect the product to solve and the suppliers will decide how to provide it. A good example for this is software development. Let's imagine we require a new mobile app to interact with customers. We will explain what we expect from the app but we will not normally tell to the suppliers how it needs to be coded.

- **Conformance:** Conformance specifications are created when we know the details of what we want. The items can be precisely described, and the supplier will just need to quantify what will be the cost of them. A good example of conformance specifications are the glass bottles for olive oil. We normally sent to the supplier all the details of the bottles we require: blueprints, materials, inks...

As a general rule we will use conformance specifications when there is enough time and knowledge to detail and assess the services or products, and we will use the performance approach for the rest of the occasions. Performance specifications are always easier to draft and sourcing processes are easier to manage but we may have issues when comparing proposals as different providers can have very different ways of providing things.

2. Supplier Identification: Identifying suppliers is not as easy as it may seem. There are many variables to take into consideration to ensure all the different types of suppliers are assessed. Identifying suppliers is not only relevant for new supplier or competitive exercises but also to assess if the existing supplier base can be improved. We split supplier identification in 2 areas:

- **Criteria:** this is about defining the number and type of suppliers that will be invited to the RFP "supplier mix". In addition to meeting the minimum requirements in terms of product and service adequacy, there are a bunch of other things we need consider when creating a supplier mix. Some of them are: independent suppliers vs the ones that are part of a large group, local vs international, small vs large, niche/specialised vs multi-product, offshoring... Each of these criteria must be defined for every sourcing event and procurement managers needs to ensure they invite the right variety of suppliers to maximise the value. As an example if you are looking to build a new CRM capability to communicate to customers you can find a supplier that provides the entire process or you can go for a solution to build your audiencias directly form you database, then another supplier to provide the platform to create the campaigns and finally another one to do the SMS and email delivery. One single supplier versus 3 smaller ones. Procurement managers must be supplier agnostic an ensure all options are assessed to maximise the value.

- **Scouting:** Once the criteria has been defined, this is the actual process of identifying the suppliers and getting their contact details. In the era of technology there are no longer secrets about how to identify suppliers. The main sources we use today are: search engines, speak with your network, social networks, B2B directories, forums, trade shows...

3. Request & receive proposals and assess them: Any process which involves competition will require fluent and transparent communications to suppliers. We will need to share with them the requirements, get their proposals, assess the proposals and the suppliers, select the one we believe better fits the needs and negotiate the final commercials. We have got various options:

o **RFI:** Request for Information. This is when we need more information about suppliers before inviting them to submit a proposal or when we need more information about the required products because we are not ready yet to draft the specifications and shortlist suppliers.

o **RFP:** The Request for Proposal can either follow an RFI or be the main and only process. In an RFP we will share the specifications with the suppliers and they will respond with their proposals which among other things will at least contain the services description (how they plan to deliver the service or product) and the commercials.

o **RFQ:** The Request for Quotation is similar to the above but mainly focused on getting commercial proposals.

Competitive processes require objectivity when comparing suppliers and they should be run by procurement with impartial inputs from the BU.

In addition to appraising the proposals in terms of quality, cost and product/service delivery, we also need to do a risk assessment to make sure that the suppliers won't represent any risk to the company. This will require the supplier to provide plenty of corporate information. It is normally called pre-contract appraisal and some of the main checks are:

- Financial assessment to check the supplier's financial stability.
- Data protection and information security assessment.
- Sustainability checks.
- Business contingency plans in case anything unplanned occurs.

Any competitive exercise needs to be approached with TCO eyes. TCO stands for Total Cost of Ownership and it means we need to ensure all the costs have been loaded and the comparison between suppliers is been done on an objective basis. In my career I have seen, and I have made several mistakes because not looking at TCO. Common issues are comparing products with different Incoterms,

41

exc.VAT prices vs inc.VAT prices, forgetting to add some of the transportation costs, not counting with implementation costs or using the wrong FX to compare suppliers. Any mistake caused because we are not considering all costs or because we are not comparing apples with apples will ultimately turn up into an inefficient decision. We will see TCO in detail in the Commercial Excellence chapter.

4. Negotiation: Negotiation is the last step of any competitive process. The RPF process must help us to get to the negotiation phase in a very strong position because on one hand the supplier will have accepted most of our terms already and on the other hand we will have alternatives.

In the last couple of decades technology has made less personal the negotiations. In today's world we have got plenty of e-bid tools that allow us to run e-auctions or sealed envelopes and can avoid having a direct encounter with suppliers. Auctions can get you to the cheapest provider for a specific service or product, but they can also force participants to reduce the cost in a way that may become unsustainable in the future.

5. Contract: After selecting the supplier, the last stage of the process will be to finalise the negotiation of the contract terms. In this stage we will involve the legal teams from both sides. We will cover the main clauses that procurement cares about in later chapters but there are 2 main tips that procurement professionals always need to remind.

1 – when running RFPs… it is very useful to send a draft of our contract to the potential suppliers and get them to accept the terms in order to submit a proposal. This will give us some power when negotiating the contract and will allow us to exclude suppliers that cannot deliver under the terms we require.

2- engage with your legal team as soon as you can. Legal reviews take long and the soonest you kick them off the earliest they will finish.

Please note that all the above is indicative and varies depending on the company. Sourcing is a very broad area that needs to adjust its operations to the company's needs however the key principles we have discussed in this chapter are quite common across all procurement functions.

10.Contract Management

Contract management is to me the easiest procurement pillar although it is also one of the most valuables. We define it as the process of creating, approving, signing, storing and monitoring contracts. Please note that the negotiation of the terms of the contract is not part of contract management, it is part of sourcing and it is led by legal with inputs from procurement for the commercial aspects of the contract. Contract management has the following responsibilities

1. Draft and update templates:

This covers the creation of contract templates to be used by sourcing. Depending on the size and nature of the organisation the company will have a different number of templates. A company with around 50 contracts a year can have a single template for all types of services/products that can be bespoken for every deal. A large organisation, with hundreds of new contracts each year, will aim for optimising the time of its sourcing and legal managers and will create plenty of templates. This list of templates can include:

#	Paper	Type of procurement
1	Master agreement / Framework	Direct
2	Master Agreement / Framework	Indirect
3	Statement of Work (SOW)	Direct / Indirect
4	Service Agreement	Indirect
5	Product Agreement	Direct
6	Creative Agency Agreement	Indirect
7	Licenses Agreement	Indirect
8	Sub-contractor agreement	Direct / Indirect
9	T&Cs – normally included the PO	Direct / Indirect

Large organisations operating in many markets and requiring translations can have tens of templates. It is very important to understand when each of them shall be used.

2. Contract Processes:

This is about establishing the process to connect with legal to: decide which contract will be used, negotiate with the terms with the supplier, and get it signed. Please note this is not about negotiating the contract but creating the process to do so. This process may include the creation of contract approval forms that will be completed and approved by the budget owners, procurement and legal before a contract is sent for signature. Smooth interactions with legal is one of the key success factors to build a strong contract management function and an efficient procurement function.

3. Signature

Getting the contract signed is not normally as easy as anyone who's never done it may think. The first step is to create an approval matrix in which depending on the value and risk level of each contract the signatories will vary. Then it is about managing the signature. It can be done offline or via e-signature. Getting contract takes long and sometimes the services require to be kicked off ahead of the signature. In these occasions we can use a Letter of Intent that will be followed by the contract.

4. Contract repository

This is the core of contract management. All contracts need to be saved in an online platform so that sourcing managers and BUs can access them quickly. Each contract will be stored in its own workspace highlighting the main terms so there is no need to open the actual PDF. The minimum information we suggest adding in the summary is:

- Effective date
- Termination
- Type of contract
- Termination for convenience
- Commitment
- Payment terms

- Annual value and contract value
- Stakeholder (internal & external)
- Payment terms

We always recommend creating a naming convention, so all contracts follow the same format.

5. Reporting

The reporting activity is very linked to the accuracy and details we get when storing contracts in the online repository. The more fields we add to each contract workspace the better reporting we will have. Reporting needs to be run periodically although we will also get numerous ad-hoc requests.

One of the most powerful things of contract monitoring is that it enables sourcing managers to identify the contracts that are expiring soon so that they can manage the renewals on time.

It may also allow procurement to monitor and match contracted spend with actual spend.

Ad-hoc contract monitoring is related to sporadic projects that the company may decide to run, and which will require inputs from the contract reporting team. This can be related to payments terms in case we want to increase them, spend under commitment in case we want to do a short-term cost improvement or any other thing.

11. Supplier Management (SRM)

Supplier Management or Supplier Relationship Management (SRM) or Vendor Management is the ongoing exercise of managing all the interfaces between our company and the suppliers with the aim of ensuring an accurate and riskless delivery of goods and services. In easier words, it is about knowing enough about your suppliers to be confident they won't become a risk and they will deliver as contracted. It normally has 3 key pillars.

1. Performance monitoring.
2. Risk management...
3. Supplier development.

1. Performance monitoring: The objective of monitoring performance is ultimately to avoid incurring into costs due to not receiving the services or products that were agreed or in the way they were agreed. To do so we need to:

o ensure suppliers deliver at the agreed quality and quantity levels (performance management)
o ensure the supplier delivers at the agreed costs (commercial management)

Performance monitoring is normally done by the business unit with procurement support in the way of ongoing business reviews where both parties will assess the performance of the supplier and compare it to the specific expected levels agreed in the contract. In order to be successful there are 3 things that need to happen:

• **Service Levels Agreements (SLAs):** SLAs set up the minimum level of performance we expect the supplier to deliver. These indicators need to be objective and clearly defined in the contract so we can measure the supplier against them. An example of an SLA can be a 48h delivery time from requisition. Every time the supplier delivers in more than 48h they will be breaching the SLA.

- It needs to follow a **structured framework** agreed by the parties which contains: the recurrence of the assessment (quarterly, monthly...), the stakeholders and their responsibilities, and the format (checklist, tests, surveys...)

- **Incentives**: the supplier must have incentives to overperform. These can we in the way of positive rewards (performance related bonus) or negative rewards which are also known as service credits (supplier liable to remediate any lose we can make because of them underperforming or breaching the SLAs).

2. Risks Management: Risk Management is the process of assessing suppliers in a regular basis to minimise the likelihood of a risk event happening and be prepared in case it happens. We differentiate 2 phases depending on whether the contracts have been signed or not (pre-contract and post-contract). In the pre-contract stage, the focus will be on gathering information to avoid on-boarding a supplier which can become a risk while in the post-contract stage we will focused on ongoing checks of existing suppliers.

Risk management requires a structured process that sets up the framework that will be used to identify, assess, quantify, monitor and mitigate risks. We have seen before how it is normally done by either the BU or specialised teams and how to be successful supplier risk management programs require a structured process which looks at the supplier from 2 angles: value (cost of the products/services) and risks. It normally has the below 3 steps:

- Define risk segments
- Segment suppliers
- Assess suppliers

- **Define risk segments:** We would need to define what is considered a risk to the company and then create different levels of risks so that suppliers can be segmented and not all of them are assessed in the same way. Assessing suppliers is time consuming and we need to prioritise depending on their particularities. A very simple example of how the risk segmentation matrix can be done is shown below. For each type of risk we are defining 3 levels depending on the impact: high, medium and low.

Type of Risk	High Risk	Medium Risk	Low Risk
Financial	Annual spend >£100K	Between £50k and £100k	<£50K
Quality	Supplier providing goods or services that can materially impact the final good or service provided by the company	Supplier providing goods or services without which the company will face delays or additional costs	Any other type of supplier
Supply	Supplier providing goods or services without which the company won't be able to operate	Supplier providing goods or services without which the company will face delays or additional costs	Any other type of supplier
Information security	Supplier having access to the company's systems and data	Supplier having access to the company's facilities	Any other suppliers

In the above example we have only used 4 examples but there are more types of risks (e.g. Data Protection, Sustainability, CSR…). Each company will need to create its own bespoke risk management models.

- **Segment suppliers:** Once we have defined the types of risks, we will need to agree how are we going to segment suppliers. The easiest way is by transforming the above into questions and sending them to the BUs. Depending on the answers to those questions, the suppliers will be automatically classified into high, medium or low risk. Following the above example, the questionnaire could be something like the below:

Type of risk	Questions	Answers High	Medium	Low
Financial	What is the annual cost of the service?	>£1000k	>£50K	<£50k
Quality	Is the supplier providing anything that can materially impact the final product/service provided by the company?	Yes	Yes	No
Supply	1. Is the supplier providing goods or services without which the company will not be able to operate? 2. Will the supplier provide goods or services without which the company will face delays or additional costs?	Yes to 1	Yes to 2	No to 1 and 2
IT security	1. Will the supplier have access to the company's systems and data? 2. Will the supplier have access to the company's facilities	Yes to 1	Yes to 2	No to 1 and 2

This exercise will classify suppliers into different risk levels.

• **Assess suppliers:** Following the supplier segmentation it will be time to run and maintain the risk assessments. The programs will vary depending on the risk of each supplier because we won't conduct the same checks for someone that has been classified as low financial risk only than to a supplier which scored high risk in all areas.

To do the risk assessment we will need to plan the tasks that will be undertaken for any type of risk, the stakeholders responsible for those tasks as well as the recurrence. See below an example:

50

Type of risk	Risk assessment checks		
	High	**Medium**	**Low**
Financial	- Do not make upfront payments. - Assess financial stability - Identify an alternative supply to deliver them 10% of the volume	- Identify an alternative supplier - Assess financial stability	Nothing
Quality	- Deep quality management - Heavy SLAs and Service Credits in the contract	- QBRs (Quarterly Business Reviews) - Stock monitoring	Nothing
Supply	- Ongoing business contingency plans - In-plant FTE provided by the supplier - Heavy SLAs and Service Credits in the contract	- QBRs (Quarterly Business Reviews) - Stock monitoring Business recovery plans	Nothing
Information security	- Review supplier policies - Run penetration test - Physical audit	- Add clauses to the contract - Regular checks	Nothing

The process we have described it is called pre-contract risk assessment because it happens before a new supplier is onboarded. After the contract is signed, a similar process called post-contract risk assessment will be kicked off and it will be focused on updating and monitoring the checks previously done. We will need to define the recurrence that each of the checks in the table above will require.

3. Supplier development: This is the last but not least bucket of the SRM activity, and it aims to improve the value we get from the supplier. Some of the things it may contain are:

o develop the supplier to improve quality and delivery.
o new product development (create new products to be ahead of competition)
o efficiency identification (incentivise the supplier to identify ways to achieve cost savings).

I like to say that the three above can be defined as innovation management and resource improvement.

The responsible for SRM vary significantly depending on the company but we can assume that procurement will at least be the one setting up the corporate supplier management framework and managing the systems required to undertake an accurate SRM. Then some of the specific activities can be handed over to the BU, compliance, risk or any other teams...

As it happened with the previous pillars SRM can be run using the most common tools like email, excel... or can go through specialised software which will automatically define roles, identify tasks and timelines and trigger the communications to the responsible of each step.

12.P2P

P2P stands for Procurement to Pay and it covers all the processes between raising a PO and making the payment to the supplier. In some organisations it is managed by procurement and in some others, it is managed by Finance. It is commonly seen as the most administrative component of procurement, but it is a very important activity and needs to be managed effectively. Delays in payments or POs will end up in category managers receiving plenty of emails from internal stakeholders and suppliers and ultimately spending a lot of their time solving the issues.

The phases of P2P are:

1. **Request and Create POs** – A PO (Purchase Order) is a document issued by a buyer to a seller that states the basic terms (quantity, goods and services description, delivery timelines, price…) agreed by the parties. Although it is not a contract as such, most laws understand POs as a contract by its nature so it is important we understand that when we are sending a PO to a supplier we are effectively committing to certain products/services. As a general rule there are 2 types of POs that may be requested:

   o **Standard PO**: Which at least includes the tracking number, supplier name, client name, amount, payment terms, service description, delivery date, shipping instructions and payment terms. In addition, when possible we will include our standard terms and conditions in the reverse of the PO so that in case there is no contract in place, we can enforce our standard terms with the supplier.

- o **Blanket PO or Opened PO:** It only includes a broad description of the services and there is a fixed delivery date. It is normally used to avoid raising plenty of POs for recurrent costs. e.g – if we are using a consultancy to which we are going to pay £1m a year split in 12 equal monthly payments, there is no sense to raise a PO every month. What we will do instead, is to raise one blanked PO covering the entire year. In these POs the delivery time and service/product description will be broader or even undefined, and we will exclude the cost as we don't want to make any commitment.

The first step to create a PO requires to raise the service/product request. This is done by the person who owns the service. Once the PO request is raised it will go to the approval flow which at least shall include the below 3 different type of departments/stakeholders. Depending on the level of spend of each requisition, the seniority of the approver will vary. It is also P2P's responsibility to create the right approval matrix.

- **Finance** – to approve that there is budget for the specific purchase.
- **Procurement** – to approve that the supplier has gone through the right procurement process, the supplier has been assessed, there is a contract in place and the price is the correct one.
- **Business Unit** – the budget owner within the business unit requesting the services/ products to approve the spend.

Once the requisition is approved the PO will be created and send to the supplier. Most companies operate "no PO, no Payment" procurement model. This means that unless there is a valid PO the internal stakeholders cannot request anything to suppliers. With no PO no payment approaches, the internal stakeholders are educated to raise POs ahead of starting with the products or services. If the supplier delivers a service with no PO there is very little leverage in case things go wrong or we believe the pricing was not the right one.

2. **Invoice** - Once the PO has been raised, the supplier will deliver the product/service and then submit an invoice.

- **Reception:** The invoice is nowadays received by email to a standard email address and normally processed for approval and accounting.

- **Receipt:** In indirect procurement the most common approach is that goods/services are receipt by the BU after receiving the Invoice. The invoice is sent to the requisitioner for review who needs to confirm they are happy with the delivery or challenge any discrepancy. This is normally known as Goods Receipt. In manufacturing or distribution goods are normally receipt in the warehouse and it can be done ahead of receiving the Invoice by issuing a document to the supplier acknowledging the goods have been received and receipt. This normally happens in the warehouse via the Inventory Management or Warehouse Management systems and it is done by the supply chain or logistic teams.

3. Payment: Once the Invoice is receipt and depending on the payment terms of the supplier, the payment will be released. Payment terms are important to manage cash. It is not the same to pay within 7 days from the date we receive the invoice than paying within 100 days. I spoke with the CPO of a groceries retail chain who explained that they had an average payment terms of 80 days with their food suppliers. They were getting cash from the customers in the stores and then paying suppliers 80 days later which gave them the chance to use the liquidity to generate additional revenue streams through their treasury department. Planning cash upfront is key to do not get into financial troubles.

It is important to mention that P2P is a process rather than a technology although there is software specifically created to manage the entire P2P process or components of it. In addition, almost all ERPs can cover the entire process however depending on the nature of the company it may be preferable to use niche options.

13.Procurement teams

When structuring a procurement function there are 2 main questions that need to be answered:

1. How are we going to allocate the resources?
2. What is the right level of centralisation/decentralisation?

The most common options about how to allocate resources are:

- **By Business unit:** Each business unit across the company will have its own specific procurement resources.
- **By location:** Each country, market or region will have specific procurement people dedicated to them.
- **By project (Project Procurement):** The procurement resources will be allocated on a project by project basis depending on workloads and the complexity and adequacy of the project.
- **By category (category management):** The teams will be created depending on the type of the services and products being purchased.

Below we can see a table comparing the advantages and disadvantages of each option:

Type	Advantages	Disadvantages
By BU	• High stakeholder engagement at a BU level • High visibility on the spend and budget • Good understanding of the business	• Lack of specialised knowledge • Low visibility across BUs
By Location	• High stakeholder engagement (market/BUs) • High visibility on the spend and budget • Good understanding of the market	• Low visibility across Markets • Lack of specialised knowledge
By Project	• Ability to deliver on time • Close monitoring of projects	• Low visibility on business and category
By Category	• Cross company visibility • High knowledge of the commodities within the category	• Lack of stakeholder engagement (market/Bus) • Heavy workloads with multiple projects

The level of centralisation is the second point to be considered when creating procurement teams. There are various options:

- A **fully centralized** procurement function is the one where all the procurement resources (teams) report directly into the CPO. No matter whether they seat in the markets, in the BUs or they are structured by categories the entire procurement team will report to the CPO and will be an independent team by itself.

- A **fully decentralised** function instead, is the one where the buyers don't report to the procurement function. We can have buyers within the markets reporting to the local's MDs or within the different departments reporting to the heads of the department. In this occasions the common approach is to do not have a global CPO.

We also have lots of hybrid of models in between. Each organisation needs to understand its unique needs and then adequate accordingly the structure to ensure it works efficiently. In fact, hybrid models are the most common structures I have seen over the last years in large organisations.

A very common approach for large, multi-market and multi-product organisations is to have a central procurement function that reports to the CPO complemented with local buyers based in each market that report into the local market. In this type of structures, the connection between the global and the local teams is key to ensure the success of the function.

14.Category Management

Category Management is the approach used to organise procurement teams depending on the nature of the products or services required by the company. The way it works is that the range of products purchased by the company are broken down into groups (categories) of similar or related products. These categories normally match the spend hierarchy we have seen in the spend taxonomy described on the Spend Analytics pillar. In category management, specific procurement teams will be then allocated to manage each category.

An example of a very basic category management structure is shown below. It only has 6 categories but helps to understand how it looks like top level. Note that category management applies to all three types of procurement: direct, indirect and product buying.

Type	Category
Indirect	Technology
Indirect	Marketing
Indirect	Corporate Services
Direct	Packaging
Direct	3rd party Manufacturing
Direct	Materials

The key thing of this approach is that each category will have its own dedicated team. In the above example there will be a category management team for technology, another one for marketing and so on. In small and medium companies, the responsible of each category is called Category Manger while in large organisations, due to the size of the supplier base, various category managers may work in the same category and report to the Head of Category or Category Director.

Category management approaches have become the most common way of operating procurement functions in today's world, due to the benefits it creates versus other structures. The main benefits are:

1. It enables category manages to acquire a strong market knowledge around the specific commodities under their scope.
2. Stakeholders within each business unit have a single point of contact.
3. It empowers category managers to have full visibility of the spend companywide and empowers them to leverage their procurement decisions on behalf of the whole organisation.

We can look at category management as the natural evolution of sourcing. In addition to being focused on single-commodity, immediate or short-term events, category managers also care about the long-term strategy of all commodities within the category, changes on the demand and some aspects of SRM. It is also the natural evolution for the members of the team. sourcing managers once have acquired the right experience and skillset, tend to jump to category managers roles.

The responsibilities of a category manager go beyond the pure sourcing activity. We can assume that a category manager needs to cover all 5 sourcing pillars, plus in addition, be responsible of some specific activities to this role.

Procurement pillars:

1. **Sourcing:** Overseeing all sourcing events for the specific category. Identification of opportunities and long-term planning.

2. **Spend analysis:** the role of the category manager can go beyond the usual spend analytics expectations. They are normally part of the budgeting process, spend monitoring and on-going reporting.

3. **Contract Management:** monitor contract expirations and increase the spend under contract for the specific category.

4. **SRM/ issue resolution:** category manager needs to maintain a fluent communication with all material suppliers. It is very important that this communication is aligned with any other form of communication that other teams have with the suppliers. We expect from category managers to: on one hand run or oversee the

supplier assessment and performance review programs, and on the other hand to resolve any potential issues at the supplier end (quality not in line with the contract...) or at our end (massive delays in payments...). In addition, they also are intended to facilitate conversations around initiatives to improve efficiency or drive innovation.

Specific to category management:

In addition to the pillars the category managers will also be responsible for at least 3 other things:

1. Strategy and planning
2. Stakeholder management
3. Market knowledge

1. Strategy and planning: This goes beyond the sourcing strategy we have seen as part the sourcing cycle. While a sourcing strategy impacts a single project/commodity, category strategies make impact to the entire category. Having the full picture and control of a specific category allows category managers to plan forward and create and implement long term strategies. There are plenty of templates and mechanisms out there to create category strategies but to me the key thing to always consider is that procurement category strategies need to be aligned with business goals. Category managers need to see theirselves as if they are efficiency consultants that support the business to achieve their goals in a simpler, faster, and most efficient way. Building business cases to explore new ways of doing things or alternative business models to mitigate the cost of externalities is the day to day routine in any successful category management function. Senior leadership will use these inputs to take strategic decisions.

An example I faced some years ago, was the case of a very large multinational ecommerce that wanted to reduce the marketing costs, particularly the ones related to creative and communication agencies. We assessed all the different options and evidenced that the most valuable alternative was the creation of a centralised in-house creative studio from where designers employed by the company were going to create banners, posters and any other communication asset required by the brands and markets. My marketing category manager created the business case analysing the current situation (current agencies, current costs, quality requirement, number of assets required per year...) and the comparison with the in-house option (salaries, technology, new facilities, processes...). The case was presented to the leadership who bought it and asked us to move to the implementation phase. These types of initiatives are broader than a single sourcing process as they hit multiple commodities and suppliers, impact internal processes, and take a lot of time to implement. In the example I have used, we needed to align all current contracts with agencies so that they terminate when the internal studio was fully operative, we needed to source the technology needed by the sourcing team, we found specialised marketing recruiters to build the team as well as the facilities where they were going to operate from. In parallel, the marketing team designed a new briefing process, reporting mechanisms and the communication plan. All together in conjunction made the project very successful.

Another good example was the case of a pharmaceutical organisation that had some issues buying certain type of raw materials from European suppliers due to a new regulation. Asian supply was available but from when the new regulation was released the prices there went up significantly. With this in mind we created a cross functional team which included the procurement category manager, product marketing, R+D, manufacturing... to discuss alternatives. The final business case had 3 objectives: 1) move to an easier and cheaper to source raw material in the space of 12 months, 2) Minimize the impact of the cost increase and ensure supply during these 12 months. With this in mind the category manager created the long-term strategy with specific actions for short term (bulk buying to existing supplier and over stoking to reduce cost and ensure supply) and mid/long term (sourcing new suppliers to deliver the new materials once R+D defined them and develop existing suppliers is possible).

2. Senior stakeholder management: There are 2 main objectives around stakeholder management: satisfaction and engagement.

The main thing to avoid is the BU bypassing procurement and doing things their own way, and to do so, we need to influence stakeholders by evidencing the value that procurement can deliver. The "bypassing" is more common in indirect procurement however I have seen it many times in all types of procurement.

The first step to achieve successful stakeholder management is about identifying the stakeholders. Depending on the type of procurement the stakeholders may vary:

Type	Main Stakeholders
Direct	R+D, Manufacturing, Operation
Product Buying	Sales, Product, Operations
Indirect	It depends on the category – Chief Marketing officer, Chief technology officer…

.Then the second stage is around identifying what is their view of procurement and what is level of satisfaction. Some of the complaints we may hear are that procurement slows things down, they are full of processes and forms, they are too focused on costs, they lack knowledge on the business…. In my career, I have seen them all. I have even worked in a company in which in my first day, one of the closest stakeholders literally told me he was not waiting for me, the company was not waiting for me and that they could do very well without any help from procurement. One year later the same person wanted one of my team members seated next to them full time because he was very happy with the partnership. Changing stakeholder's perception is possible and the way to do it is by applying the right balance between persuasion and concessions.

We need to focus on obtaining quick wins that will highlight to the stakeholders how we can add value. At the same time, we need to make some concessions and don't force stakeholders to follow our advice until they come by their own after having seen the value we deliver.

The conversations with the stakeholders need to happen top down. We require the entire organisation to connect with procurement and follow our processes and the only way to get there is by influencing the most senior members of each business unit so they can channel their teams through procurement.

The recurrence of our interactions with stakeholders it's also an important point to plan. The more senior, the less we will interact with them, but still important to update them from time to time and escalate in case there a material issues. I always try to use the below table which has 3 levels, and although it varies a lot between companies it helps to plan the communications accordingly. Below there is an example using the type of stakeholders we can have if we are sourcing promotional stands for a make-up brand.

Level	Function Owner	Budget Owner	Service Owner
Stakeholder	Chief Marketing Officer	Retail Director	Trade Marketing Manager
Description	Head up all marketing teams and functions	Oversees the operations of trade marketing as well as other teams	In charge of the day to day operations
Topics	We will share the main issues and achievements for all the projects under his remit	We may cover other projects under his scope	We will cover only this project in detail
Interaction	Sporadic	Medium	Frequent

3. Market knowledge: Being organised by categories gives category managers the opportunity to acquire excellent category knowledge. We need to be aware of the latest news in the market, new products/services, merges and acquisitions related to large suppliers, new regulations and best practices across competitors. There is plenty of content available today and we may become very inefficient if we don't have not some kind of structure in place. Structing what content are we going to access and the frequency of it, will give us a routine that will enable us to be efficient in the time we spend with learning. Some simple sources of information we have got today are:

1. Blogs/magazines or newspapers specialised in the commodities we are in charge of or in procurement as a whole.

2. Events related to our categories.

3. Regular meetings with the BU leaders to see what is going on their minds and where they want to take the function going forward.

4. Networking with colleagues from other companies.

5. Training sessions with the suppliers to understand new products/services or to increase overall knowledge.

6. Professionals associations.

Finally, it is worth to make a point around the specific skills that any procurement professional requires, in order to step up to a category management role. As said, we understand this type of roles as the first management level within procurement and the gate to progress up to the top of the procurement organisation. In addition to all the "must have" analytic, results driven and project management skills we also require:

- Team leadership and management skills

- Strategic thinking: understand and aligning with BU goals, long term thinking plus ability to set up and deliver ambitious objectives.

- Ability to challenge and question the status quo and to adjust to business requirements.

- Excellent synthetisation, presentation and communication skills in order to influence senior stakeholders.

- Fast thinking. In particular with everything related to commercials, prices, budgets and capacity to identify opportunities at a macro level.

15.Procurement processes & policies

The procurement process is the set of steps and rules that anyone within the company must follow when intending to buy to 3rd parties, goods or services that will enable them to meet their business goals. The purpose is to guide anyone internally to complete the acquisition of any service or product they may require. We have already seen some of the steps of the corporate buying cycle in the Sourcing and P2P chapters. Below the extended version which contains all the steps. Our procurement process will need to walk stakeholders through each of the below which may or may not be needed depending on the commodity and the company.

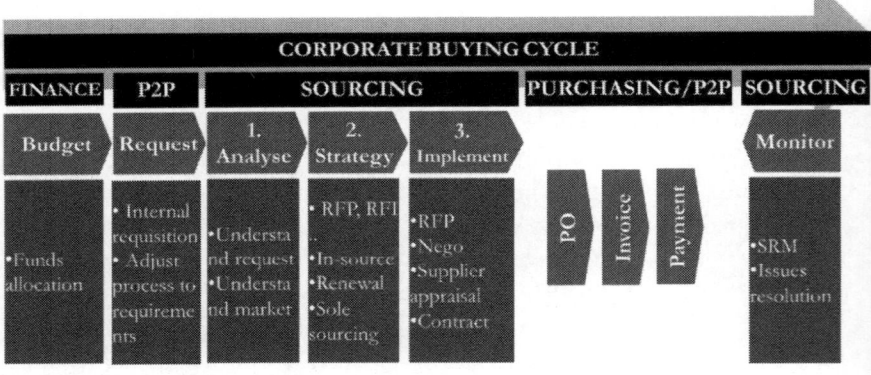

Any procurement process needs to meet 5 requirements:

1. **Feasibility**: ensuring we have got the right systems and resources to fulfil all the steps of the process.
2. **Consistency:** The process needs to be able to be applied to the entire organisation.
3. **Agility:** Time efficient to help people wasting the less possible time to go through the process and it do not slow things down.
4. **Effectiveness:** it needs to be designed for a specific set of purposes which are: risk mitigation, time effectiveness and cost consciousness.
5. **Update:** It needs to be reviewed and updated frequently.

We have said several times already that the main purpose of procurement is to drive value so when creating a process it is always important keep it in mind. We want to avoid creating things that will create confusion and additional work instead of helping the company to improve its operations.

In order to understand the need of a procurement process it's important to understand first how small actions can make big wins and how the company needs to care about any single spend item. Let's use as an example the below company for which I worked as a consultant few years ago:

Turn over	£3.5b	Actives Suppliers	13,000
3rd party spend	£1.8b	Annual transactions (invoices)	400,000
Markets (with offices)	23	Employees allowed to raise POs	6,000

In the above scenario we see how important it is to understand that every single penny counts. Saving £2 from each transaction could increase the profit of the company by £800k a year. On the other hand, with such a large volume of transactions and suppliers it is key that the procurement process is agile enough to don't disturb the operations.

The main role of the procurement process is to allow colleagues internally to make efficient purchases by guiding and supporting them through the buying cycle in order to generate value by minimising costs and risks. For those that are new to this world, in simple words, the procurement process will need to tell people what to do when they want to buy a new thing.

The process also varies from company to company and may vary too depending on the type of commodity (direct, indirect or distribution) but below we can see a very summarised top-level process.

Level of spend	Type of Supplier	Type of service	Risk level	Procurement involvement	New Supplier Appraisal	Approval required	Contract Required
Below £50k	New Supplier	New Service	Low Risk		X	Level 1	
			High Risk	X	X	Level 1	X
		Existing Service	Low Risk		X	Level 1	
			High Risk	X	X	Level 1	X
	Existing Supplier	New Service	Low Risk			Level 1	
			High Risk			Level 1	X
		Existing Service	Low Risk			Level 1	
			High Risk			Level 1	X
Above £50k	New Supplier	New Service	Low Risk	X	X	Level 2	X
			High Risk	X	X	Level 2	X
		Existing Service	Low Risk	X	X	Level 2	X
			High Risk	X	X	Level 2	X
	Existing Supplier	New Service	Low Risk	X		Level 2	X
			High Risk	X		Level 2	X
		Existing Service	Low Risk	X		Level 2	X
			High Risk	X		Level 2	X

I won't get into many details on the above, but it is important to mention that there are 4 main triggers:

- New or existing cost
- New or existing supplier
- Amount
- Risk

With these 4 things in mind we will be able to channel the stakeholders through the right process. The best way to approach the process is by asking questions in an easy to respond way (online tools, e-requisitioning tools...) so that they can self-assess what the requirements are and follow the steps easily.

Think of a large decision tree that varies depending on the answer. This is exactly what our process will do. It needs to be strong in its back office but also easy to communicate and to navigate by colleagues. The more intuitive and user friendly it is, the better.

In addition to the above the process may also vary depending on the commodity. We may want to add a 5th trigger because some companies have specific processes for some commodities. See some examples below:

o **Office Supplies:** some companies create an online catalogue with all the available items (pens, notebooks...) and the users order directly from there.
o **Raw materials:** with some recurrent, strategic, core, large suppliers we may have blanket POs in place and a speedy process to request items via an intranet, web interface....

The system we will use to set up the procurement process varies a lot. In small organisations everything will be done by email and in large mature functions there will be a requisition portal, catalogues and other tools.

A requisition portal is a site where stakeholders go whenever they have a request. They fill in with the details of the good or service they require, then the system will ask them some questions and will channel them through the right processes. It may put them in touch with sourcing in case it is needed or directly channel them to the PO requisition page in case sourcing, legal or any other function is not needed.

We have described the procurement process so now we need to focus on the **Procurement Policy** which is de document where we will capture all the steps and rules above mentioned. The Procurement Policy goes beyond the procurement process and sets out all the principles that govern any acquisition of goods and services as well as interactions with suppliers. Some of things it includes are:

- Procurement Process
- Code of conducts with 3rd party engagements
- SRM programs
- Spend Approval Matrix
- Inventory levels
- Contract requirements

When crating a policy, we need to make sure at least 4 things:

- It is accessible to everyone – normally stored in the intranet.
- It is communicated properly – everyone who has access to suppliers is aware of the policy.
- It is supported by the senior stakeholders – normally approved an enforced by CEO or CFO.
- It is reviewed and updated frequently.

16.Creating functions from scratch

At this point we know enough to be able to create a procurement function/team from scratch. Sometimes we will join companies where there is already a procurement function in place, but that does not mean we cannot improve it. Creating a procurement function also involves expanding and updating the existing ones.

We will explain below the key things to consider when creating one from absolutely 0, so you will need to cherry-pick what best works to your organisation depending on your level of maturity. It is important to mention that ahead of creating anything, the first thing when joining a company, is to run a quick procurement audit to see the current level, strengths and weaknesses.

In order to create a function from scratch we will follow a very similar process to what we have been doing in the rest of the chapters; which will be looking at the type of procurement, the procurement pillars and the procurement taxonomy.

1. Assess requirements – The first thing is understanding why we have been hired and what is the outcome the CEO, CFO, COO or the person that has decided to create the procurement function expects from it. They may have decided to build a function to obtain savings, to minimise risks, to streamline processes…It is key to understand the role procurement should play in the organisation.

2. Spend Gathering – we will not be able to build a spend analytics function in our first weeks, but we can have an idea of the last year spend by speaking with finance and trying to get a quick snapshot.

3. Suppliers segmentation: once we have got the high-level view on the spend it is the time to segment our largest suppliers. We normally follow the Pareto 80/20 principle. It is used in procurement to do supplier segmentation and it assumes that roughly 20% of the suppliers cover 80% of the spend. This 20% includes our core suppliers with the largest spend and the ones we should prioritise. Supplier segmentation also helps to identify the size of each spend category.

4. Stakeholder identification: is about identifying who will be our core stakeholders and connect with them to identify how procurement can add value to their functions. Stakeholders can be part of the core business or from other support functions like finance, legal, logistics or compliance.

5. Building a team: with all the above we will have an initial view around what resources (team) we will require and how are we going to structure the team (by categories, by location…). It is then time to draft the job descriptions and start recruiting.

6. Create the process & policy: we have seen how important is to create a process that ensures a smooth buying cycle so at this stage we will be able to start with the basics and add on from there.

7. Build the pillars: we have talked about the procurement pillars extensively already. This step then will be around building all the sub/functions within the procurement team: sourcing, spend analytics, contract management, SRM and P2P. Each of them will require its own strategies and processes.

8. Select technology: each of the pillars may require a specific set of technology. We will cover this later on the technology chapter, but it is very important to select the right type of technology that fits in each organisation.

9. Connect with suppliers: most provably some conversations with suppliers will happen from day 1 to resolve issues or manage urgent things but at some point, we will need to build a plan to keep communications fluent at least with the core ones.

10. Agree reporting: once the most important things are ready is time to agree reporting with our senior leadership.

Creating a function is like building a house. It can become extremely messy so we will need a detailed plan mapping all the steps we are going to follow. There are plenty of things to be done so prioritisation is key. No matter how hard we work or how smart we are, it will require time to get the full function up and running, so identifying what goes first will release pressure at the time we get valuable quick wins. I have draft below an example of a priority plan.

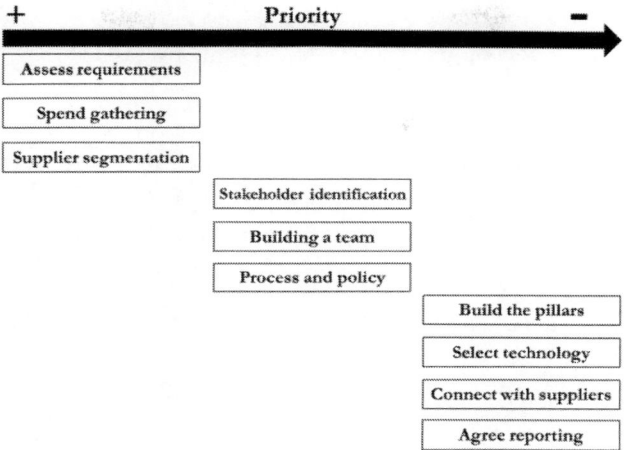

Some of the things we are going to require may come with a cost (resources, technology, travel...) so it is also important to get full visibility on the total costs the function is going to have. We can also prioritise activities by the value for money each of these activities is going to delivery.

17.Driving Synergies

In today's world most large organisations have achieved their size and market share via a combination of organic growth (increase sales...) and external growth (merges, acquisitions and partnerships). The role of procurement in M&As is key in order to ensure we are buying at the right cost, identify synergies and implementing them.

The most common ways of fixing the price of a company is by looking at the profit (EBITDA...) and applying a multiplier. To give an example (at a very high level), if for example a company has a profit of 10 a reasonable price can be 50 (5 times the profit).

Whit this is mind when doing one of these deals it is important to:

1. Ensure we will preserve the pre-deal value of each of the companies (don't lose)

2. Try to increase the value of the new organisation by identifying synergies (make a profit)

Looking at point 1 above, there are plenty of unsuccessful M&As in the recent history of management. You just need to type "unsuccessful M&As" in the searcher engine and you will get plenty of articles. This happens when the value of the new company is lower than the value that the 2 companies had before the merge or acquisition and it can be related to a wide variety of reasons we won't cover in this book.

Our focus is going to be on point 2 "increasing the value" by identifying synergies. As per Cambridge's definition a synergy is the combined power of a group of things when they are working together that is greater than the total power achieved by each working separately. This is exactly the role that procurement plays in M&As. Identifying ways were the 2 companies together will do better than each of them in isolation and implement those ways.

The fact we can incorporate the new company into our systems and processes and identify cost synergies will ultimately translate into the new company having reduced unit costs. That means that we are buying a company at a lower cost than what it is worth it. Let's use the IT platform of a travel agency as an example.

Company A is a big travel agency that is trying to acquire company B which is a smaller operator. Company A has its own IT platform (Self Booking Tool from where the customers can book hotels, flights...). It has developed it over the years with internal resources while company B uses a third party. The cost of this 3rd party is not fixed. The supplier charges a 3% on each transaction done via the platform. Let's have a look at company's B P&L summary.

Annual data	Company B pre-deal	Company B post deal
Revenue	100	100
3rd party cost	60	57
salaries	25	25
Profit	**15**	**18**
		+ 20%

In the above table we can see how integrating company B in the company's A proprietary platform and subsequently terminate the contract with the external supplier will increase the profit of company B by 20%. This means that we paid for a company that was priced at a profit of 15 when we will be getting a profit of 18. In other words, by identifying the synergies we have bought it cheaper.

Another good example I have faced few times happens when a company has its own factories, but they are operating with significant spare capacity. Then they acquire another company that produces the same products but uses a 3rd party manufacturer because they don't have their own facilities. By adding the new company to the spare capacity, they will not only save the mark-up of the third-party manufacturer but also reduce the impact that the fixed costs of running the factories have into the price of the final product.

There are 2 phases where procurement support is required in M&As:

Pre-deal:

Due diligence: The first thing is to obtain information about the company we are going to acquire or to share information about both companies in the case of merges. This requires accessing sensitive information like contracts with 3rd parties, business processes and spend data. When this info is needed, the deal has not been signed yet so to avoid issues with confidentiality we normally create "clean rooms" where people from both companies' shares information. Please note this rooms are now digital (shared folders, FTPs…). Everyone with access to the information will sing an NDA and will use it for the purpose of the acquisition/merge only. The main objectives of the due diligence are:

- Asses there are no issues with the contracts with core suppliers (long term commitments, exclusivities, prices that are above the market average…)
- Identify potential cost savings from synergies and quantify their value.
- Define goals and taxonomy.
- Review the procurement structure and systems and define how will we set it up the procurement function post-deal.

Post-deal: Once the deal has been signed it is time to identify the initiatives to drive synergies and deliver them.

1. Identify initiatives: Some common examples of potential ways of obtaining savings from M&As are:

- o **Consolidate spend at a supplier level:** when we have various contracts with the same supplier, and we want to consolidate them into one to benefit from volume.

- o **Consolidate spend at a service level:** when various suppliers are providing the same service/product and we want to consolidate with one of them to benefit from volume.

- o **In-source:** when one of the companies has a specific activity/function in-sourced and the other one uses a third party and there are chances to use the internal capabilities for the group at no additional cost or at a lower cost than the 3rd party.

- o **Elimination of redundant work:** when the service/product is purchased twice and there is only the need to do it once. A good example of this are information services. If one of the companies buys a specific market report, no matter how many new companies we acquire, if they operate in the same market and require the same report, we will only need to buy it once.

- o **Improved asset utilization and productivity:** this is similar to consolidating services but focused on CAPEX spend – factories, logistic platforms, offices…

2.   **Deliver synergies:** In order to deliver the synergies a plan needs to be created. If there is no structured process to monitor progresses and to challenge any deviations, then the expected synergies are at risk. The plan must include at least the below:

- o Expected goals.
- o Stakeholders, roles and responsibilities.
- o Budget in case there is any investment needed.
- o Reporting mechanisms.

It is important to note that while we will be focussing on 3rd party spend, the same exercise will happen from a HR perspective with the aim of identifying synergies across the employee base.

Depending on the market the ability of a company to acquire business and efficiently and quickly embed those business into the organisation can make the difference with competitors and give competitive advantage.

Even when we are not managing any acquisition it is important to set up the things internally ready for potential acquisitions that have not be explored yet.

76

This applies to every single aspect of the organisation, but it is very important when taking spend decisions or signing new contracts. When the entire company works in a way that everyone is operating as if new merges and acquisitions are going to happen soon, integrations will take less, and the value will be released sooner. The ability to assess a company, identify value and quickly integrate it into the current group so that synergies are realised quickly is what I call the Buy and Plug approach.

Buy and Plug is basically the approach were the entire organisation is set up in a way that new acquisitions are constantly been expected and everything is set up in a way that facilitates the integrations. Contracts are flexible to add volume, teams are ready to pick up new tasks, facilities have spare capacity or plans to obtain it if needed, the systems can handle new instances...

18.Procurement Technology

We commonly refer to procurement technology as e-procurement. This chapter is split in 2 parts. The first one is around selecting the right level of technology and the second one is about the different types of technologies we can use to improve our procurement functions.

1. **Identifying the right technology level:**

It is commonly assumed that technology will save time and although sometimes it may be true, it does not always happen. In 1980s financial auditors didn't have excel or any of the sophisticated tools they have got today to do their calculations. They used to do everything manually in books and when excel was released in 1982 everyone thought it was going to change radically the way they worked, and they were going to reduce their workload significantly and work less hours. As everyone knows this has not happened, and even we know excel streamlines significantly the things they did manually before, it has also created additional responsibilities and requirements. I wanted to use this example to highlight that it is very important to keep asking to ourselves "why" we need the tools before deciding to implement any technology. If we cannot proof the value, then there is no point to do it. Using emails to run RFPs, excel to create spend reports and shared folders to store contracts can be the right choice for some organisations which won't get any value from investing in more sophisticated tools.

2. **Types of procurement technology:**

The technology we have got available to support procurement can be classified within the procurement pillars. Some of the tools can be used for specific tasks only, whereas some others cover all 5 procurement pillars.

- **Spend Analytics:** we have discussed this in detail in previous chapters. This can be done with the more common tools like excel, using a data visualisation engine or implementing a purposed build tool. The key functionalities are around displaying spend data and classifying it by categories and some of them also include the ability to compare spend vs budget. The latest trend is to add artificial intelligence to enable the tool to automatically classify suppliers, identify spend deviations and opportunities to consolidate.

- **Sourcing**: e-sourcing tools allow to run sourcing exercises like RFX (umbrella for RFP, RFI, RFQ...). Some of the tools have e-bit options (electronic auctions, sealed envelopes...) and even the capability to automatically compare proposals. They are a very good option for companies that run multitude of tenders and want to follow a standardise process and keep everything within the records.

- **Contract Management**: technology supports contract management in 3 different ways:

    o **Contract repository**: to store the contracts, monitor terminations and create reports.

    o **Contract building and templates**: to maintain and update templates. Some of them include collaboration tools that allow us to share the draft with the supplier and track changes and I have recently seen a couple tools that just by entering some basic information about the services in scope can build the entire contract automatically.

    o **e-signature**: to allow electronic signature and avoid hard copies.

- **Supplier management:** Supplier management software supports all SRM tasks, assess supplier risks and monitor performance. These tools allow to send questionnaires to the BU, to segment supplier depending on the risk and to request information from the suppliers to assess them.

They also allow to communicate effectively with suppliers and stakeholders, manage timelines, monitor performance, request information and store it as needed.

- **P2P:** P2P has plenty of software under it. The main purpose of it needs to be the automatization off all processes between requesting a service/product and making the final payment. Some of the tools we have got out there are:

  o **E-ordering:** e-ordering is used to streamline the procurement process and take off some workload from the procurement team. We have seen it in the chapter about the procurement process, and this is about creating a tool that will guide internal requisitioners across all the steps they need follow to acquire a specific product/service. E.g. for a recurrent low value good/service with an existing supplier, the tool may take them directly to the end of the process (sending the PO to the supplier) whereas for a new, large, strategic service the tool may put them in touch with the right sourcing manager. E-ordering is to me the hottest topic now in 2020 as it really can streamline all the interactions between procurement and the BUs. Think of it as if it is an online page where everyone that wants something goes to see what are the steps to follow. They answer few questions and the tool will guide them through all the relevant processes that are required before they can send the PO to the supplier.

  o **POs**: we have talked a lot in the P2P module. This is about rising the requisition, approving it, creating the PO and sending it to the supplier.

  o **Invoicing**: Automation and receipt of invoices. Today most of the tools allow to automatically digitalise the information contained the PDF invoices. Once it is entered into the system, the service owner will need to receipt it so that the payment can be released.

- o **E-payments**: bulk payment releases. This needs to match with the payment terms of each supplier. From my experience, it is very common to keep payments within the ERP instead of using specialised tools.

- o **Expense Management:** expenses that employees make and claim back to the company (travel...).

- o **Inventory Management:** control stocks, warehouse and returns oversight.

Although some people put them under sourcing, I like to include within P2P the below tools. To me they are not part of the sourcing process but the result of it and this is why I think they need to go under P2P.

- o **E-Catalogues & integrations with suppliers:** e-catalogues are sites in which employees will see all the products that have previously agreed with a supplier/s for a specific category and they will be able to place orders directly from there. They can be powered by the supplier or they can be part of our e-procurement tools. An example of this are office supplies (notebooks, pens, pencils...). We may agree a catalogue with specifics items and pricing with a supplier and then the supplier will create an online catalogue from where our colleagues will order.

- o **Market Places:** These are the same type of e-commerce sites than the ones we use as individuals to buy things online but specific for B2B. There are plenty of them and we normally use them for non-core, nor risky, low value spend.

- o **Buying syndicates:** A buying syndicate is a third party that consolidates volume from various buyers to obtain a cheaper cost in the supply market. It can be done at an industry level (car manufacturers consolidate volume of a specific good they need) or at a commodity level (a buying syndicate specialised in utilities where any company can take part of it). A good advantage of buying syndicates is that they screen the suppliers upfront so if we are conformable with their level of screening, we don't need to screen them again. In addition, they will send us a single invoice instead of one per supplier.

o **ASLs / PSLs:** Approved Supplier Lists or Preferred Supplier Lists are lists of suppliers that have been pre-qualified and with which the requisitioners can get in touch directly for the specific purpose each of them has been pre-approved.

The final point is around Integrated Tools. These tools (normally well-known ERPs) can cover various of the above and some of them can cover all the steps. It is a good option for large organisations because there is no need to integrate plenty of different tools and the information is coming from the same source however their cost is higher. The fact that all the systems are in the same platform can save a lot of time which will be translated into a lot of savings at the end of the day. It is very important than before taking the decision to consolidate procurement technology with a specific supplier, a business case is built to assess pros and cons and assess what will bring more value to the company.

19.Commercial excellence

Commercial excellence is something that all procurement professionals will and must develop during their careers. I have been asked a few times by BU leaders the following question: do you think your guys will do better than mines? My answer has always been that, my guys, with their inputs, will get us to a better outcome than their guys in isolation. The reason why is because this is what we do all the time, what we have been trained for, and what we are measured against. Driving value through commercial efficiency is the core of the procurement business.

Commercial excellence is about don't missing any fact or opportunity and delivering projects to the highest standard. I divide it into 4 main areas and every procurement professional must have a strong control of all 4:

1. Cost Drivers
2. Pricing Models
3. TCO
4. Sourcing Alternatives

We have already said many times how important is to challenge and question the status quo to ensure we are not missing any opportunity to increase value. Reviewing these 4 points ahead of taking any decision will help us to take efficient decisions.

1. Cost drivers: Cost drivers are all the factors that will make the price of a product or service. Understanding cost drivers is a must before we can undertake any sourcing activity. To identify cost drivers, we need to see all the costs that the supplier incurs in order to provide the goods or services and what is the impact that each of them has in the final unit price we pay. At the end of the day, a supplier (like us or like any other company) is an organisation that incurs in costs to create a product/service, then adds a mark-up and sells it to clients. This means that the costs incurred by our suppliers are going to have a direct correlation with the price we will pay for the product. I like to make my suppliers feel like if my customers are their customers, and we both are just different steps of the goods and services value chain we saw in the introduction. Cost drivers vary depending on whether we are buying goods as raw materials, finished products for distribution or services but, as a general rule, we have got 3 types of cost drivers:

- **Supplier driven cost drivers:**
  a. Raw materials, semi-finished and finished goods
  b. Logistics, production and operation costs
  c. Labour
  d. Overheads
  e. Mark-up
  f. Taxes

- **Market driven:** There may be externalities that impact the cost of a good/services. Fuel price fluctuations in case of transportation, political problems in the main country that produces the raw material or a natural catastrophe that stops a specific industry for a while.

Knowing with details what are the cost drivers, and which and how can be manipulated to reduce cost and/or improve quality, will help during the negation process. We should know how the price reacts to any alteration to the cost drivers.

2. Pricing Models: It is important to do not mix cost drivers with pricing models. The cost drivers are the factors that impact the supplier and ultimately make the price of the good or service. The pricing model instead, is the criteria the supplier uses to establish a price for their products. Sometimes the costs drivers match quite well with pricing models and some others don't. E.g. when we go to a restaurant the main costs drivers are the quantity and the quality of the food, the staff and the location. In case we choose an "all you can eat" restaurant then the pricing model is a fixed fee but If we go to "a la carte" restaurant then the pricing model is quality and quantity because each plate has its own price. In the "all you can eat" one there is no direct connection between the cost drivers and the pricing model although most probably the owner will be averaging all the costs, adding a mark-up and dividing them by the number of expected clients to fix the price. In the "a la carte" restaurant there is a direct connection between the cost drivers (cost of the raw material and quantity) and what we pay for the meal. Both buyers and suppliers need to control well cost drivers and pricing models.

The main pricing models are:

o **Fixed fees:** when no matter the usage we make, we will pay always the same. A good example of this is the rent of the offices. It may be based on location or square meters but in the leasing contract we never link the price to those variables. We just pay a fixed monthly rent.

o **Output-based (quantity and quality):** this is the most common pricing model whereby we pay depending on what we get, either quantity, quality or a combination of both. There are plenty of examples. Almost everything in raw materials and distribution is priced this way.

o **Success fee:** This is based on performance. It is quite common in digital marketing. Some companies have affiliate programs to increase acquisition. Affiliates are 3rd parties that acquire/send new customers to the company and get a % of the incomes coming from those customers. If they don't send any customer or if the customers, they send don't buy anything, then the affiliates don't get paid.

o **Hybrid Models:** A combinations of the above

The difference between the above pricing models' seats in the level of risk each party is willing to take. In the below chart we can see how the risk of each of the pricing models we have described changes depending on whether we look at the supplier or at the buyer.

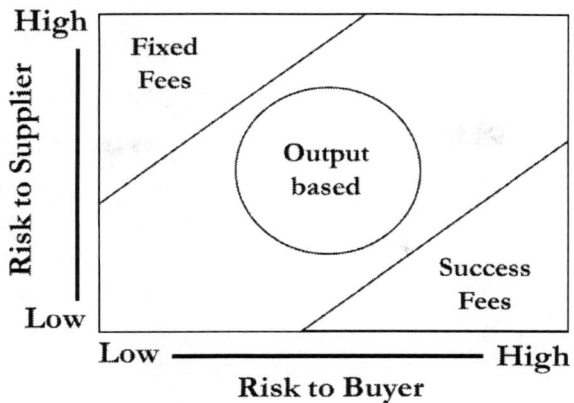

With fixed fees we are taking the risk (we guarantee business to the supplier) so we can negotiate a lower rate. With variable models it works the other way around. Understanding volume fluctuations and supplier performance is key to select the right pricing model.

If we look at direct procurement the most common mechanism is the output-based model, however we may also see fixed fees. In 3rd party manufacturing, sometimes, the company pays a fixed fee to the third party for the production of the goods and provides all the raw materials and components required to do so. What the company is actually paying, is a monthly fee to rent the factory, the labour and the related costs.

In distribution we can normally see either output based models (we buy upfront what we are going to sell to our customers) or success fee models whereby we get the goods and services and we pay them to the supplier once we sell them.

Finally, indirect procurement is the one that has the broadest variety. We can see fixed pricing, output based and success fees. In addition, it is worth to talk about Open Books approaches which are quite common in outsourcing and people-based services. With this model the supplier agrees to deliver a specific service. They share all their

86

costs with us and then we apply a mark-up. The points of negotiation in this instance are the cost efficiency of the supplier and the mark-up.

In addition to the pricing model there are other things we need to consider:

o **Volume thresholds**: for output based pricing models we will often see that the unit price varies depending on the total volume. When we hit a certain level of volume then the price goes down. There are 2 types: the one where the reduction will be applied to the incremental volume only, and the one that once we trigger the reduced price, it will apply retrospectively too.

o **Variable bonus:** some services have a variable bonus depending on the supplier performance. This incentivises the supplier to perform well. The only downside is that the metrics that will trigger the payment of the bonus need to be very objective, and it may require a lot of monitoring and communication.

o **Rebates:** volume rebates are a % of what we pay to the supplier, that is paid back to us when we hit certain level of volume. Volume rebates work in the same way than the volume thresholds above explained. Once we hit the volume to trigger the rebate, it can apply to the incremental spend only or to the entire spend.

3. **TCO:** It stands for Total Cost of Ownership and it is basically the process of understanding all the costs we will incur when buying something in addition to the actual cost of the product or service. In too many occasions we have decided to acquire things and afterwards we have received a surprise when a hidden cost that was not assessed before raised. TCO it's important because of 2 things:

o It avoids cost surprises and ultimately value reductions.

o It helps to compare apples with apples when evaluating multiple sourcing alternatives (make or buy, different suppliers…)

Some of the key things we need to consider when building a TCO model are:

Cost	Description
Good/service cost	The actual cost of the service or product
Sourcing Cost	Hours invested in the sourcing activity if done internally, or external cost if a 3rd party does it.
Maintenance	One product may come with free maintenance whereas another one may not have it included.
Depreciation	Some items depreciate faster than others, so we need to look at residual value.
Transportation	The location of the supplier, the logistic costs and the rest of transportation terms may vary among suppliers.
Risk Management	Different suppliers or sourcing options can bring different levels of risks.
Labour Cost	We may require hiring people to run the product/service.
Financial Costs	Payment terms and payment conditions (fractioned payments...) can impact significantly.
Warranties and Insurances	If we need a certain level of warranty and a supplier cannot provide it, we may need to get it externally at a cost.
Storage	Storage has multiple options. One supplier can store it in their warehouse and ship directly, whereas others can send it to our hub. Different options will have different costs.
Environmental impact	Environmental costs are normally related to reputation impacts or fines.
Scrap	Scrap cost is important mostly for machinery and facilities.
Returns	In distribution, the cost of returns is material, so if the sellers allows us to keep returns it may have an impact on costs.
Taxes	Taxes may vary among suppliers. This is normally related to the location of the supplier.

4. Sourcing Alternatives: As we have said before, sourcing is not only about finding suppliers. There are 3 different types of sourcing options and it is important to consider all of them before undertaking any project.

External sourcing: this means sourcing products and services externally is the most common approach to benefit from the volume, and avoid increasing in direct costs.

- **Single supplier:** a single supplier can be the best option if we need to build a very close relationship, or if there are economies of scale or monopolies.
- **Various suppliers:** multiple suppliers are normally used when we need to secure the supply in case one of the suppliers fails, or if we want to put pressure on the suppliers to increase performance.
- **Outsourcing:** this is the process of giving to a single supplier an entire function currently done internally or currently delivered by several suppliers. It is good to transform fixed costs into variable, benefit from expertise, and be able to manage additional work in peak times.
- **Supplier pool:** we may define a set of 3 or 5 suppliers that will be briefed every time we have got a request, and award the services to the one which offers the best value each time.

Internal sourcing: in-sourcing may be the right option when there is additional value versus external supply. This happens when we have a lot of volume and want to reduce costs, when the activity is core and want to increase control, or when we want to improve delivery timelines.

- **Make it entirely:** this means we will hire the team, buy the equipment, and create the required processes to in-source the specific product or service.
- **Partial making:** this happens when we keep some of the resources with the suppliers, and bring some others internally. Let´s use a call centre that is currently provided

by a third party as an example. We may hire the team to run the call centre internally but keep the telecom system with the supplier that was providing the full service previously.

- **Make it via a third party:** we can use a third party to provide the specialised team to in-house what was provided externally. An example of this is when we in-source part of the legal activity, but instead of hiring the team from scratch, a legal firm provides full time in-plant lawyers.

No sourcing: no sourcing happens when we identify a way to terminate the purchase of the product or the service without impacting the operations.

- **Demand management:** understanding the amount purchased or requested to the supplier and matching them with the internal needs and the volumes coming from other sources of supplies, often highlights unnecessary costs.

- **Process reengineering:** by improving a process, we may identify products or services that are not needed. I have helped a couple of times companies to optimise their minimum unit of sale to save money in packing.

- **Substitution:** this happens when we identify other resources, either already available in the company, or provided by a third party, at a cheaper cost that can meet the business requirements. In today's world it is common to use technology to automate tasks that were previously done by suppliers.

20.   Contracts

I am not going to get into lots of details around contracts, otherwise we will require a book just for that. I will rather focus on reviewing what is a contract and what does it imply, and then what are the key things we need to care when creating contracts.

A contract is any type of agreement between 2 or more parties that can be enforced by law. To us, from the procurement angle, contracts will normally be in the form of written documents that will detail at least, the services/products to be provided, and the price of those. Contracts are made of clauses and there are 2 main types of clauses: the ones that can be managed by procurement with very little or no support from legal "commercial terms", and the ones that require legal inputs "legal terms".

It really varies depending on the commodity and the industry but below we can see the main commercial clauses we need to ensure that appear in all of our contracts:

- **The parties**
- **Term and termination details:** effective and termination dates as well as early termination clauses.
- **Purpose of the contract:** description of the products or services in scope.
- **SLAs:** The Service Level Agreements are the minimum levels of performance we expect from the supplier. They must be monitored closely.
- **Delivery terms and timelines: we** buy in-puts that are used to create the final out-put we sell to customers so making sure delivery is done on time and as agreed, is key to do not impact our operations. Delivery details include the form, place, manner, and time in which suppliers will provide the products/services.

- **Cost, Currency and payment terms: the** more breakdown we add around cost the more leverage we will have in case we want to add or remove products or services from the contract.
- **Governance:** it is important to establish what papers will govern the relationship. We normally send a PO to the suppliers containing standard terms on it. Then they may reply to the PO by adding their terms in the sales acknowledgment or invoice or some other commercial reply form. This will create confusion around what terms are the ones that apply, and it is called "the battle of the forms". The best way to avoid this is to state in the contract that it supersedes any other document, and that any changes need to be made as a contract addendum.

Legal terms are not in the remit of procurement and should always be reviewed by a specialised lawyer. Below an example of some common legal terms:

- **Intellectual Property:** To make sure that any names, designs, products, materials, and images created by the supplier for us is owned by us.
- **Data Protection:** these clauses are key in the era of the digitalisation because we hold, and we share, plenty of sensitive data. There is specific regulation in these regards.
- **Liabilities:** when one of the parties accepts to be held liable for the losses and damages incurred by another party
- **Indemnification:** these are contractual obligations to reimburse the other party if a specific liability arises. They normally cover specific risks and are linked to the liabilities clause above. They can be easily enforced.
- **Warranties:** this is an assurance of the condition of the products, services or some aspects of the supplier. They tend to be more difficult to reinforce as failure to meet a warranty is normally managed as a breach of contract and can allow to terminate the contract.

- **Insurance** – level of insurance hold by the supplier.
- **Applicable law** – country of jurisdiction.

The above list sets up the basis of the relationship. It is important to note that failure of the supplier or the buyer to meet any of the clauses stated in the contract, will be a breach of the contract, and will allow the other party to terminate it and claim indemnifications if applicable.

We have described some of the main clauses but there are plenty of them. No matter the type of service or product, to me there are 4 key clauses that procurement managers need to consider in every contract:

- **Termination for convenience:** this clause allows the parties to terminate the contract giving notice with certain time advance.
- **Commitment:** this clause may oblige the parties to keep providing and/or buying the services to the other for a specific period or time or a specific amount.
- **Exclusivity:** this clause may restrict the ability of the parties or one of them to do business with a different party for the same purpose.
- **Upfront payments:** paying before the service/product is fully delivered

To me if we have the right to terminate a contract with let's say 1 month notice, there is no volume commitment and there is no exclusivity for us to use the supplier, then as far as we haven't make any upfront payments, the contract has very little risk because we can exit it immediately.

On the other side, if we are using a supplier with which we are not happy, but the contract has no early termination clauses, we have committed to a certain level of volume, there is exclusivity and we have paid upfront the entire year, then there is no way we will be able to exit even when we are not happy.

Understanding these 4 clauses and managing them strategically will help us to don't be in a uncomfortable situations in the future.

When entering into contracts it's important to make a good balance between, do not putting the company into a big risk, and giving confidence enough to the supplier to delivery well and give us a good price. We also need to think about creating something that is flexible enough to do not add workload or slow things down.

21.Negotiations

Negotiation technics and tactics is something that will be bespoken to every individual. Each of us needs to create its own way of negotiating from the experience and learnings. I like to see how negotiation approaches are very different amongst the members of my teams, and to be honest, I like the fact they do it differently as far as they are fair with the suppliers and the internal stakeholders, they achieve the goals we set and they don't expose the company to any risk.

What really needs to be standardised, or at least structured, is the process that is followed when running a negotiation. Negotiations have evolved to a place where we use plenty of technology, and there is a lot information accessible to both parties. We are no longer in 1980s, and today negotiations don't happen in dark smoky rooms as appears in the movies.

The use of technology on one side has increased transparency and price accuracy with things like e-RFPs or e-auctions, which reduce a lot the traditional negotiation role made by the buyer. On the other hand, technology has made communications much easier and cheaper thanks to tools s like email or videocalls.

We are not going to go through negotiation tactics in this book, but we will talk about the main stages I believe any negotiation must have:

1. Pre-negotiation
2. In-negotiation
3. Post-negotiation

Let's look with more detail at how we approach each of them.

1. Pre-negotiation

- **Data Gathering:** There is always going to be information which is unknow (supplier mark-ups, production processes...) but the more information we have, the stronger position we will achieve. The minimum information we require about the service/product we are going to discuss is:

  o Product details / service breakdown
  o Volumes (historic and projected)
  o Previous spend report
  o Contractual terms

- **Planning:** no matter the format we use (spreadsheets, presentations, word...) we need to build a plan ahead of any negotiation. To do it, we need to 1) assess the information, 2) define objectives and 3) create the story. It needs to be a story/case that makes common sense to the supplier. They need to understand our rational, feel that our approach is fair and then buy it. The more data and evidences we provide to build the story, the easier it will be for the supplier to accept it. Below you can see a list with some useful items to build negotiation cases and identify levers.

  o Do we still make the same money out of the product/service we produce with the supplier inputs?
  o Do we have the breakdown of all the services provided by the supplier and their costs?
  o Do we have a usage report? Has the usage decreased?
  o Have we increased the volumes? If yes, did we receive a discount to the unit rate or a rebate?
  o Has the supplier underperformed or overperform?
  o How easy is it to find a replacement?
  o Is the supplier having less costs or more incomes by any chance?

96

- o TCO - Have all the costs been accounted and is the supplier aware of them?
- o What is our weight in the supplier customer base?
- o Can we add a rebate?
- o Can we offer to do an early renewal?
- o Do we know the impact that raw materials have to the final cost?
- o Can we run an internal and/or external benchmark? Is the price fair?
- o Can we make it, outsource it or offshore it?
- o Can we cancel the services/products? Do we need them?
- o Are we buying too much? Or too good?
- o Are we asking the supplier for services which add little value but add costs?
- o Are we paying a premium for any reason?
- o Has the supplier provided any ideas for cost reduction? Does the supplier have incentives to lower costs year over year?
- o How does the cost compare to our budget?
- o Are we obsolescing items before they are used?
- o What is the supplier position? What are they going to ask and what will they respond to our comments?
- o What is the pressure at the supplier side?

Once the negotiation case is built, it is helpful to share a summary with the supplier to let them know where are we coming from, so they don't get surprised and have enough time to digest and prepare accordingly.

No need to mention that the objective of a negotiation is to get into an agreement that works for both parties, otherwise we will be imposing our criteria and there is no need to negotiate. On one hand we need to make sure the supplier is flexible and willing to improve the relationship and on the other hand we need to put ourselves in the supplier skin and don't try to obtain things we know are not fair or feasible.

- **Alignment:** everyone who is going to be part of the negotiation process at our end needs to be align regarding the goals we want to achieve, and the reasons why we want to achieve them.

2. **Negotiation:** as said this is not a book about how to negotiate but I am listing below the main things I always try to keep in mind when negotiating.

   o **Listen** – the 2 parties need to interact. The more they talk, the better for us.

   o **Mutual understanding** - Show the other person how their needs will be met.

   o **Concessions** - Don't give anything away without getting something in return.

   o **Goals** - Never be afraid to ask for what you want. Pursue your goals if you think they are fair.

   o **Walk Away** - Always be willing to leave or postpone.

   o **No rush** – Focus on the supplier pressure instead of ours.

3. **Post-negotiation:** the process does not finish after the negotiation. There are a couple of things we need to make in order to don't get surprises.

   o Send minutes to ensure everything has been properly understood.
   o Bank achievements and communicate the agreed next steps.
   o Align with internal stakeholders.

As said at the beginning, this book intends to be a complete but summarised guide to procurement.

Complete in the way I have tried to cover all the main areas I believe anyone who is in procurement needs to control, and summarised because I have tried to keep them short and straight to the point.

I cannot stress enough how rewarding it is to be part of well-structured and successful procurement functions. This profession gives us the chance to maintain a holistic view in almost all the areas of the company at the time we keep a direct connection with the outcome of our work and how it impacts the bottom line profit.

I need to clarify that there are no content references or bibliography because all the content is unique, and has been created by myself from the notes and learnings I have taken during my career.

Hope you liked it and please feel free to leave any feedback at www.aboutprocurement.com.

Many thanks,

Alberto Menen.

Printed in Dunstable, United Kingdom